Co̶n̶

Ham

THICKNESS BY SOCIAL CLASS

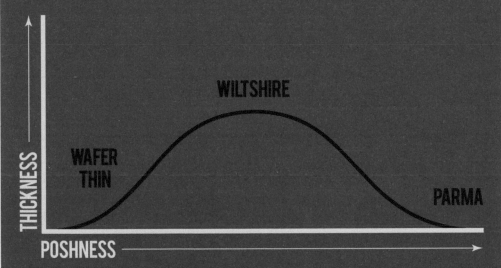

THANKS

Thanks this quarter to Andrew Northrop, butcher to the gentry; Dr Christina McLeish for continued support; and Marina O'Loughlin and Tracey MacLeod for perceptive analysis and great taste. To Lucas Hollweg for holding down two back-to-back doubles, and to Natalie Whittle for being an excellent boss.

To Adam Gopnik for introducing us to Elizabeth Pennell, and to Elizabeth Pennell for reminding us that every meal should end with 'a spirit, to cleanse, and an oil, to soothe'.

We still can't thank Fi KirkP enough.

This issue was brought to you by Bath buns, cheese Doritos and a fanatical devotion to Antica Formula.

Editor: Tim Hayward

Sub-Editor: Fiona Kirkpatrick

Design and Art Direction: Rob Lowe
(rob@rob-lowe.co.uk)

Printing: Buxton Press

Published by Funistrada Ltd.,
51-52 Trumpington St.
Cambridge CB2 1RG.

Reproduction of material is strictly prohibited without prior permission. All rights reserved. © Funistrada Ltd.

Set in Gill Sans and Perpetua

ISSN 2042 1109

Hancock's LUNCH HOUR

Thomas Blythe

I can clearly recall my first encounter with Tony Hancock.

It was in the back garden of the house I spent my childhood in and must have been somewhere around the summer of 1978.

I lay in tall grass next to the deckchair in which my Dad, in his flared jeans and pale blue shirt, took sips from a warm can of Bass ale between belly laughs, as we listened on his old Roberts Radio to *Hancock's Half Hour*.

Whatever made my Dad laugh made me laugh as well, and through my teens and into adulthood I found myself listening to Hancock's radio shows and, later, watching the television series, over and over.

What's brilliant about watching *Hancock's Half Hour* today is that, like the Ealing comedies, it offers a delicious glimpse back into the social life and mores of Britain – or in Hancock's case, East Cheam – in the early 1960s.

There's one particular episode of the show in which our hero gives the modern day viewer a taste of a London dining experience now lost to most – the public canteen.

In *The Economy Drive*, Hancock and Sid James – his on-screen housemate and inveterate worst enemy – arrive home from a three month trip around Europe to find James has forgotten to cancel the bread and papers, turn off the lights or tell the milkman they won't need any delivered. 'All that milk gone to waste! Sixteen pound ten of bottled cheese out there.'

Resolving to cut spending, Hancock declares 'no more posh restaurants. The Dorchester is out. From now on, nothing over three bob', and on his way to buy a suit for a meeting at the BBC from the Post Office lost property department (what chance these days I wonder) calls in for lunch at what the original script by Ray Galton and Alan Simpson describes as 'a self service cafeteria (a replica of Lyons)'.

Lyons Corner Houses were hugely popular in London, as were copy-cat establishments further afield in the home counties. The first opened in 1909 and the last finally died out towards the end of the 70s as diners were lured to the new, exotic steak houses – Berni Inn and the like. A shame, for they catered to most, on different levels – literally, in some of the bigger sites.

The Lyons-style refectory that Hancock takes his three bob to is very much at the lower end of the scale, however; very much in keeping with his new austerity. He joins the queue with an empty tray and the hope of an affordable culinary delight from inside the pigeon-holed servery. What follows is a tremendous study of the British nature of queuing: accusations of queue jumping; jabs in the kidneys with plastic trays; an array of the class stereotypes of the day – the posh twit, the huge thuggish lout, the shrill fag-smoking counter girl – and the glorious cashier, played by Patricia Hayes, who takes no quarter and gives none at the checkout.

Hancock is led a merry dance, as each pigeonhole door is opened to reveal either nothing or a selection of wan delicacies such as meat patty and chips or mince and beans. And an 'independent fruit flan' for afters.

'I'm just not a mince and beans man. That's all there is to it. You could call it an unreasonable hatred if you like, but there it is, that's the way I'm built.'

Having ignored the golden rule of the cafeteria – if you've handled it you've got to pay for it – and after a futile appeal to the cashier, Hancock ends up with London's most expensive bread roll and marge – two shillings and sixpence (about £2.25 in today's money). As he cries, 'the one part of the meal you get for free at The Dorchester!'

Garnishing his stale roll with both tomato ketchup and salad cream, for they are free, Tony sits next to the posh twit, only to lose his hard-earned lunch when it's cleared away by the fag-toting waitress as his back's turned.

Appalled by the swimming mix of sauces *rouge et blanc*, the posh twit makes a dash for the gents, leaving his own cloche-covered lunch on the table for Hancock to scavenge. It is of course, Mince and Beans.

As traumatic as Hancock's attempts culinary thriftiness are, I can't help thinking economising in terms of dining out then seem preferable to those today. The constant prods on television for a McDonalds meal deal or a Subway special for your £1.99 simply don't hold the same appeal as meat pie and peas for two and six.

The drug-addled rock star Pete Doherty once said of *Hancock's Half Hour* 'It's certainly the language of a long gone era, if it even existed in the first place. I don't know if it's possible to be nostalgic for a time that didn't exist, but I think I am.'

I don't know much about rock music, nor have I chased the dragon like Pete, but I know what he's talking about.

You'll find us in the queue, arguing with the cashier. I'm the one in the astrakhan coat and Homburg, eyeing up the independent fruit flans. F&K

SEAL BLOOD SOUP

BRIE O'KEEFE

This is a story about my mother.

It is 1986, and we are in Qikiqtarjuaq, Nunavut, Canada, though back then it was known as Broughton Island, named for a dead white explorer who 'discovered' the place before Canada realised that maybe the places they found already had names. It is a cold place, barren and treeless, and at four years old, it is my home.

It begins with the smell of roasting chickens. I remember following the smell from my bedroom into the kitchen, where I saw three birds turning golden brown relaxing in the oven.

Normally my mother roasted chicken on Sunday, and never more than one for all four of us. I remember it was August, the end of the summer, where the temperatures peaked around 10 or 12 degrees. My mother was dressed in a thick wool sweater, our summer wear of choice when the snow had finally receded, the sea ice just barely cleared out and the temperatures began to hint at reaching double digits.

When I remarked at how delicious the chickens smelled, my mother told me not to get too excited – she was going out 'on the land' – hunting on a boat, and she was taking the chickens with her. They were going to be eaten cold later on, family style. Fingers and hands would rip the meat off the carcass, the bones being lifted away one by one; a fitting contribution to a hunting trip where the main catch would be eaten raw. In Nunavut, table manners mean large pieces of meat are raised to the mouth, bitten into and the excess sawed off, inches from your face with a traditional circular knife, an *ulu*.

I can imagine my mother's reaction when, aged 29, during our first months in Broughton, she arrived at the community gymnasium, two small children in tow, for our first community feast. She had brought a macaroni salad made simply with mayonnaise, celery and carrots. She arrived to find four large dead seals, laid out on pieces of cardboard flattened to create serving platters on the gymnasium floor. As men butchered the seals, the liver was chopped up and eaten raw, immediately, the first thing to go.

The ribs were put in large aluminium pots of blood mixed with chicken stock cubes and instant noodles and boiled to make a deep, amber stew. After the liver, chunks of meat were sliced off the carcasses and divvied out as the queue patiently passed by. Tables were lined with platters of dried meat (to be dipped in butter and eaten) and fresh char caught in the Arctic Ocean. And there was my mum's macaroni salad.

You brought your own plates and cutlery if you wanted to eat. The community was not accessible by road, meaning disposable goods were a luxury, as they were flown in and approximately quadruple the usual price. As people queued to receive pieces of raw liver, meat and dried fish they were given mugs of the boiling blood soup (or fresh blood, depending on your preference) to drizzle over everything as it was eaten. Accompanying all this was bannock, a type of bush bread similar to a scone, made by mixing flour, salt and lard and shallow frying over a campfire (or in today's case, baked in an oven).

I imagine her stopping short; unsure of whether to enter this community gathering that could so easily be the setting of a bloody Greenpeace campaigning video, all for a potluck dinner. I know from my own experiences she would suddenly be all too aware of her whiteness, of her permed hair in a town without a hairdresser. She is so different. But she presses ahead, places her contributions on a table and shoos my brother and I off to play with the other children running about. After all, she is curious, and when it comes to making friends in town, it's going to happen here or nowhere. People are as curious of her as she is of them. Although there is a shyness with the adults that is compounded by language barriers, she is made to feel welcome. She tries to joke at her own expense to move past their quiet.

So by the time I walked into our kitchen to the smell of roasting chickens, my mother knew well what her Inuit hosts would like to eat – I think they had even requested the chickens specially. So I watched enviously as she packed them away, wrapped in tin foil, and set off in the boat to hunt seal, harvest soapstone and pick blueberries.

I know that as they skipped across the Arctic sea, wind stinging, frigid water splashing, my mother found herself getting chilled. Although she was dressed in a full winter parka, rubber boots with felt lining and mittens, she couldn't shake it. A deep chill, that no amount of hot tea from her Thermos nor warm food could shift. As they stopped the boat and scanned

the waves for the telltale puff and splash of water as a seal surfaced to breathe, my mother shivered in the boat, miserable and the source of some incredulity from her hosts. It was summer! How could she be cold?

The hunter spies a seal and shoots. They pull the boat round before the carcass can sink and haul in their kill. With eyes gleaming, my mother's friend tells her she knows exactly what must be done to warm her: seal blood soup.

As they haul the seal aboard, they slit down its belly with a long knife.

The butchering is quick and efficient. As the hunters eat the steaming liver immediately — males eating in turn according to seniority, blood dripping down their chins — my mother's thoughts to turn to vampires. The visceral scene of blood is difficult for her to accustom herself to.

On a camping stove our hostess heats water, adding a North American bush classic — Lipton chicken noodle soup mix (little more than powdered chicken bouillon cubes and instant noodles) — and the entire ribcage of the recently swimming seal. When it is boiling, she mixes this 50:50 with seal blood, and hands my mother the mug.

My mother is a strange mix of disgusted, worried about being polite and incredulous that this dark red metallic-smelling mixture will have any better effect than her cups of black tea. She worries she is the butt of some joke: make the white women eat gross food. But manners win, and my mother breathes carefully through her mouth and downs the soup as best she can, her notoriously sensitive gag reflex making the process slightly less visually graceful than she would have liked. Her hosts find this hilarious and giggle maniacally.

But the effect is immediate and long lasting. The salty, hot, coppery blood is mixed with extensive fat. This keeps the seal warm and, apparently, my mother. She feels heat emanating from within her, beginning with her stomach, running straight down to her toes. She finds herself removing gloves, scarves, her hat as she physically begins sweating and steaming. She is reborn.

I remember missing my mother that day. Being only four years old I was used to her constant presence. In a town of 400, she almost never did anything without my brother and me in tow. Even my father wasn't invited on this day. It was a day just for her. I remember her returning, fresh faced and dishevelled, entertaining our relatives at home on the phone with her tales of seal blood, me sitting at her feet, listening. She brought whale bones washed ashore back for my brother and these 'dinosaur bones' can still be found in our basement.

They moved from hunting seal to fishing for Arctic char, a relative of salmon, to be dried in racks in the eternal midnight sun before being stored for the winter. They visited an island where our community had formerly been based, before they were settled by the Canadian government, given E-numbers instead of names, their children taken from them to church schools thousands of kilometres away. They were moved to a more 'strategic' location to assist the Canadian government's attempts to assert sovereignty over the North, a callous term that usually involved great losses of Inuit life.

My mother returned to us that day, warmed with seal soup and with a head full of windswept hair, reborn in the North. With seal blood swimming through her veins, she was returned home to us wild, just that little bit more *inuk* than when she had left. F & K

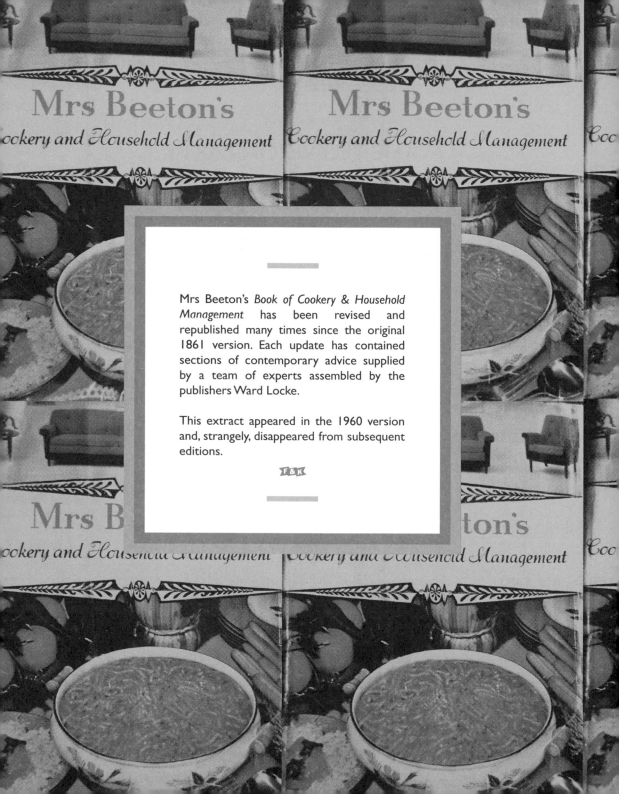

Mrs Beeton's *Book of Cookery & Household Management* has been revised and republished many times since the original 1861 version. Each update has contained sections of contemporary advice supplied by a team of experts assembled by the publishers Ward Locke.

This extract appeared in the 1960 version and, strangely, disappeared from subsequent editions.

THE TELEVISION PARTY

This type of gathering is increasingly popular, where a group of friends meet to watch some special programme or for a whole evening's viewing. The hostess will, of course, be careful to invite only people likely to be interested in the programmes in question; and she will inform them beforehand of the times of the programmes, to avoid interruptions by late-comers.

The room will need to be arranged carefully so that everyone has a comfortable seat with a good view of the set, with soft lights behind the viewers only, and with a small table for refreshments, ash-tray and so forth, at hand for each guest. Some food is usually offered, possibly in the interval if one happens conveniently, otherwise after the programmes is a good time, as there is bound to be some informal discussion of them. Sandwiches, cakes, small individual dishes of salad or some hot savoury, fruit in small dishes and tea or coffee are the usual thing, but there are no hard and fast rules and many hostesses enjoy concocting original and amusing 'television snacks'. The main practical requirement is that the food must be of the kind that can be prepared beforehand, and that the serving must be reduced to the minimum, with everything, as far as possible, already arranged in advance in small individual helpings, which can be easily handled while one is actually viewing, if necessary. Beer, cider, or other drinks can be offered or not, as liked.

UGLY
Stefan Chomka

> The UGLI fruit is a sham.

There, I've said it. It's an orange in a grapefruit's clothes. A citrus labradoodle. If it could sing (or not, as the case may be) it would be the Milli Vanilli of fruit. In short, I don't like it.

For the uninitiated, the UGLI is a hybrid of the Seville orange, grapefruit and tangerine families. But that's not why I hate it. My beef is with the name itself, which is a registered trademark of Cabel Hall Citrus Ltd, presumably dreamt up by some witty intern in reference to its less than perfect looks. Not only is it bereft of the etymological majesty of, say, the coconut – from coco, the Spanish word for grimace, thanks to its three round marks, since you ask – but its moniker is also a fallacy.

Sure, it's a little wrinkly (on the Cabel website it's pictured next to a bulldog, in case you don't get it), and it wouldn't win a symmetry competition, but on the whole the UGLI fruit just doesn't live up to its billing: viz, it gives properly ugly food a bad name.

For truly ugly food is manna of the gods: the more egregious in appearance, the more heightened the flavour. Adam may have been tempted by the apple, but he probably would rather have fallen for a passion fruit, with the outward appearance of a pockmarked ping pong ball yet filled with delicately scented, juicy capsules that explode in the mouth like flavour bombs.

Consider the shelled pistachio nut, gnarly and misshapen, with a thin brown, flaky skin as if it suffered from dermatitis, yet a flavour so subtle but rich. Or the mighty medjool date, soft and moistly honeyed despite looking like a frostbitten toe. Then there's the morel, whose brain-like appearance belies a deep, opulent flavour (the cutesy, virginal white button mushroom is insipid by comparison) and the peerless truffle – Périgord or Alba – both of which have all the natural looks of a department store beauty consultant.

The sea, in particular, is rich pickings for food that has fallen from the ugly tree. Take the delectable oyster, a morsel that hit every branch on its descent. Prise apart its knobbly, barnacled shell and you are met with a slippery, emetic embryo. So ugly is the bivalve that it often feels obliged to be accompanied by a beautiful pearl by way of apology.

Give me an Ami du Chambertin, a cheese so grotesque to behold that it's been known to scare small children, over a smooth Edam any day, or the varicose veiny Stilton, with all the *élan* of an octogenarian in a swimsuit, instead of the uniform Cheddar.

But therein lies the beauty of ugly food. It is Mother Nature's test, rewarding the eater for their bravery and optimism and poking fun at the aesthetes for their superficial stupidity. In the culinary world, he who dares, dines.

Of course, there are exceptions, such as the pulchritudinous mackerel, the beatific globe artichoke and the beguiling blackberry, but they are but few in number. If beauty is truth, then I'll have a delicious portion of lies please. And hold the UGLI fruit. F&K

Bronze, Silver and Academics

Stuart Ritson

We file in. Register is taken, giving the venue the feel of being a top London club. Or a primary school. In fact, that is exactly what is it. Men are in suits, women in dresses; some reject the formality and hide pyjamas under their black nylon robes. As we take our seats, the lights are abruptly dimmed. The glow of the incandescent chandelier, its fake plastic LED candles, is thrown onto the portraits of our college forefathers. Men in monastic robes, bursars reclining in chairs, the headshot of an archbishop placed at the top of this artists' table, all staring down at us with austere eyes. The wax tapers on the table light up the young faces around me. No doubt, in some distant future, some of these faces will adorn walls of colleges in Oxford and Cambridge.

This evening, like all too many before it, is Formal Hall. These dinners are an integral part of the history of Oxbridge and an unavoidable part of being a student there. While the novelist Vladimir Nabokov did not once look through the book stacks of the Cambridge University Library, he undoubtedly attended Matriculation, Halfway Hall and Graduation dinners. Each college has its own take on the event, but much about these meals is universal. The jerk of chairs as the students stand for the entering of the Fellows of the College, the uncomfortable silence before a solemn 'amen' as we listen for the end of the Latin motto. The affair, to those on the outside, seems deeply conservative and leans towards the Harry Potter image of Oxbridge. The truth is that the Formal Hall is far from magical, heroic or innocent.

As we take our seats, there is an unspoken acknowledgement that a game is underway. It is not normally malicious, but anyone who claims they do not want to play is met with scalding glares. It involves money, forced drinking, paranoia and a general sense of goodwill.

Take 'pennying'. It is at best a simple and very posh drinking game. It involves dropping pennies into the drinks of fellow dinners. When your drink has been 'pennied' it must be downed. However, there are more rules, and the inexperienced can quickly be caught out. A constant fear of being pennied leads players to grasp their glass; like holding onto a drainpipe during a game of Stuck In The Mud, a tight grip on the tumbler will bar others from forcing you to drink up.

After two courses and, by this point, at least two-thirds of a bottle of whatever wines your college bar happened to stock, a new part of the game begins. In a step right in the direction of stupidity, students throw five pence pieces into the custards, cakes and *crème brûlée*, all in order to 'silver' others' desserts. Instead of being required to 'down' your dessert, you are now forced to eat without the aid of cutlery. Cream-covered faces often ruin the third course for many diners.

Far from being unaware of the pathetic and childish drinking habits of the students dinning on tables laid out beneath them, the Fellows, Chaplains and Masters choose to ignore their students' pastimes. However, everything has its limits, and the ridiculous and legendary story of how Stephen Hawking became an unexpected recipient of a penny caused upheaval and the sending down of the perpetrator. As a result, a number of colleges outlaw the game, and headwaiters can be seen stalking the long tables, waiting to pounce like an examination hall monitor.

Likewise, there is a slight odour of fear emanating from those sitting near engineering students. Living up to the statistic that engineers are the most likely graduates to take part in terrorist movements, these pre-planning and over-calculating individuals have fashioned 'engineers' pennies'. Using the high tech gear provided for them in laboratories littering the city, these students have squeezed, melted and crushed pennies into a *cannelloni* shape. This aberration allows for the penny to slip into your wine bottle like the wine that will then flow down the neck of the recipient. Thus, the engineer is often the smuggest of all players.

Oxbridge has a history of drinking. If Dr Phil Withington of Christ College is to be believed, binge drinking started in Oxbridge in the 17th century. Full of young wealthy men who were suddenly freed of parental control, bingeing much in the style of the ancient Greeks and Romans they studied was a rite of passage. This in turn gave rise to a great number of 'free houses' and drinking games. Thankfully, activities like the King Street Run, in which participants drank as many pints as were pubs on one street without pissing or puking, are no longer common.

While the drunken behaviour of the student will continue to damage the name of Oxbridge, pennying is not as harsh a form of drink culture as it first appears. The wine glasses are small, and most importantly, all those taking part choose how much they are to drink. By the end of what seems a full night, we leave the dark-lit ancient hall warmed by the efforts of the chefs and the alcohol racing through our veins. In this act of sharing wine, we have been made equal and achieve nothing, which – in a place so geared toward pressure and competition – should be something worth celebrating. **F&K**

> The pudding was Jack's favourite, a spotted dog, and a spotted dog
> fit for a line-of-battle ship, carried in by two strong men.
>
> 'Bless me,' cried Jack, with a loving look at its glistening,
> faintly translucent sides, 'a spotted dog!'
>
> Patrick O'Brian, *The Ionian Mission*

Patrick O'Brian's unfinished 21 book series concerning the adventures of ship's captain, Jack Aubrey, and his particular friend and ship's surgeon, Stephen Maturin, set during the Napoleonic Wars, has gathered a large and devoted following. O'Brian's writing is famous for the accuracy of his depiction of all things naval and nautical, a literary quality not always found in historical novels, and a wit that is rarely matched. The books hold a very dear place in my heart, so much that I spent most of my third year at university, when I should have been reading Plato, Thucydides and Virgil, working my way through all the copies I could find in the local library. Not only do they satisfy the desk-bound office worker's lust for romance and adventure on the high seas, there is also a rich seam of material to satisfy even the most committed gastronome.

But how? Because these tales of blood and thunder, of fleet actions and hand to hand combat, might appear to hold little draw for this particular crowd. In fact, the whole series is an absolute treasure trove of food history: drunken dinners at sea; banquets ashore with oriental despots; all manner of familiar and unfamiliar food and drink feature. The series has even inspired its very own cookbook, *Lobscouse and Spotted Dog*, and, it seems, the menus at one or two of London's smartest restaurants (more of which later).

The books feature descriptions of food and feasts beloved of those who are familiar with them. Whether a soused hog's face, leg of mutton, a sea pie, halibut with anchovy sauce, a spotted dog (for the uninitiated, this is essentially a spotted dick), plum duff, burgundy, port, or a bottle of Château Lafite liberated from a defeated French ship, these conjure such scenes of plenty that it is impossible to read them and not feel the pangs of hunger strike.

Captain Aubrey hosts meals at sea consisting of codlings, partridge, four removes of game and figgy dowdy, washed down with an 85 Chambolle-Musigny, bosun's grog and port. He attends dinners ashore with Turkish rulers, where they dine on lamb stuffed with saffron rice (a recipe for which you can find in the Moro cookbook). He and Steven have *gigot en croûte* with French officers during the Peace of Amiens, loin of veal at The Grapes, their favourite London inn, and they even manage a *civet de lapin* when in Paris's notorious Temple prison.

So for those of us in the know, it is no accident that some of most enjoyable scenes in Peter Weir's admirable film adaption of two of the Aubrey/Maturin books, *Master and Commander* and *The Far Side of the World*, revolve around the dining table. Captain Aubrey entertains his fellow officers with an edible floating archipelago in the shape of the Galapagos Islands, with tales of Lord Nelson and terrible weevil-related puns. 'In the service, one must always choose the lesser of two weevils.'

Furthermore, O'Brian uses food to help define his characters. Jack Aubrey, whose fictional exploits were inspired by the real life actions of one Thomas Cochrane, is very much the unreconstructed dashing and heroic figure of old and a man ruled by his animal passions: fight, love, eat, drink. He is a man of appetite and 'given to worshipping his belly' (*The Mauritius Command*).

Jack and Stephen's first meal together is a memorable moment in the books, launching them into one of the longer-lasting literary friendships. Not only that, it also introduces us to some of their very favourite foods, ones which will reappear time and again throughout the books: for Jack it is a dish of soused hog's face and for Stephen it is bolets (*cèpes* or *porcini* to you and me). Stephen is a naturalist and very much taken with all types of fungi, whether it is gathering a basket full of bolets, blewits, chanterelles and Jew's ears in *The Mauritius Command* or tucking into a pheasant and truffle pie in *Post Captain*.

From this account, you might think that life in the navy was all beer and skittles, but O'Brian does not neglect to inform us of the realities of life at sea beyond truffles and claret. A brief note of caution here, because the books are novels and not a primary source on the Royal Navy during this period. However, O'Brian's scrupulous reputation in matters of historical accuracy means it is possible to tentatively draw some conclusions, which can be corroborated by primary sources from the period.

As the books show, the Royal Navy actually took great pains to ensure its sailors had enough to eat and drink throughout their long and dangerous voyages. Evidently, the food for the rest of the ship's crew did not extend to venison and vintage burgundy, but the sailor's daily ration of a pound of bread, half a pound of salt beef, half a pound of salt pork, dried peas, oatmeal, butter, and cheese was designed (within the limitations of the time) to provide enough to sustain them for their extremely physical roles. And, in relation to their daily allowance of two pints of grog (three parts water to one part rum), at least some consolation for the loss of their liberties. For the poorer crewmen, this regular supply of food was an improvement from the uncertainties on land, and there are records of Lord Nelson writing to the Duke of Clarence to express his concern over the plight of agricultural labourers in his native Norfolk.

Even Samuel Pepys, writing in the 17th century, makes reference to this in his diaries. 'It must always be remembered in the management of the victualling of the navy that to make any abatement in the quantity or agreeableness of the victuals is to discourage and provoke them in the tenderest point, and will sooner render them disgusted with the King's service than any other hardship that can be put upon them.'

However, we shouldn't exaggerate; even when the hold was full, the food wasn't much to write home about, and when it was empty, the sailors resorted to all sorts of unpalatable items. Bottom of the list was the ship's rat. Yes, the rumours are true; sailors were indeed forced to eat these when times were hard. There are even contemporary accounts of the crew using bait to 'fish' for rats in the ship's hold. There is a passage in *HMS Surprise* where O'Brian describes how the sailors would call rats 'millers', partly to 'make 'em eat better', but also because they would get dusty from their home among the ship's flour and biscuit stores. This could be an early example of that modern phenomenon whereby a Patagonian toothfish is miraculously transformed into a Chilean seabass by the simple process of being featured on a restaurant menu; unfortunately, however, I've been unable to substantiate it.

My research shows that sailors are no longer forced to eat rats, but some things never change, and the attitude to the food served in today's Royal Navy seems pretty similar to that of the sailors of Nelson's era: any deviation from the set routine is severely frowned upon. Just as the chef onboard HMS Tireless, a Royal Navy submarine, reported in a newspaper interview in 2009 that altering the routine from steak on Saturday night and pizza on Sunday would provoke a mini-mutiny, one Midshipman Gardner, an officer on HMS Berwick in 1804, states that men were actually clapped in irons for attempting to mutiny over the state of their food — specifically the scrawny bullocks that had been bought to feed them.

We can agree that the standard 19th century sailor's diet of salt pork and scrawny bullock does not have a huge amount to recommend it to the modern palate, but the same cannot be said for Jack Aubrey's favourites: soused hog's face and spotted dog. Indeed, if you read through the whole series, you could be forgiven for thinking that many of the current food trends that revolve around Britain's culinary heritage and the re-discovery of dishes from our past were partly inspired by these books.

What is remarkable is the newly found popularity of many of the 18th and 19th century dishes depicted by O'Brian; half the menu at both the Gilbert Scott (Marcus Wareing's restaurant) and Dinner, Heston Blumenthal's, could have been lifted from those very pages. Welsh rarebit (toasted cheese is Jack Aubrey's staple supper), pease pudding, salamagundy, roast halibut, mushroom ketchup, duck, trifle, and lemon suet pudding (aka spotted dog minus the spots) all feature. I even received an email from the Gilbert Scott not so long ago entitled 'Flips and Fizzes in February'; you won't by this time need me to tell you that flips feature in the books, with poor Captain Pullings laid low in *Treason's Harbour* after indulging too heavily in 'Admiral's Flip', a 50/50 concoction of champagne and brandy.

There are plenty of other dishes featured in the books from which Heston and Marcus could do worse than to take inspiration. Who could resist quaking pudding, a dessert made with eggs, cream, sherry, cinnamon, ginger and rose-water, fed to Brigid, Stephen's daughter, in *The*

Commodore; the goose and truffle pie ('more truffle than goose') from *The Ionian Mission*; or the ever-present soused hog's face, which must appear in every book in the series? Even the humble hog's face has seen its stock rise inexorably in the last few years, with pork cheeks now a regular feature on menus. Yet a whole soused hog's face might be a bridge too far for most restaurants, with sousing usually confined to herring or perhaps mackerel. This is obviously a situation that needs remedying; Aubrey's soused hog's face should rank alongside Proust's madeleine, Roald Dahl's krokan ice-cream from *Boy* and Herman Melville's Clam Chowder from *Moby Dick* in the canon of great literary dishes. What better way than to pay homage to Patrick O'Brian's literary genius than to reintroduce his hero's favourite dish to polite society?

A genuine soused hog's face is something akin to a vinegared brawn, and there is a contemporary recipe for soused pig's head and feet in Mrs Dalgairn's *The Practice of Cookery*, which was published in 1840:

'Clean them extremely well, and boil them; take for sauce part of the liquor, and add vinegar, lime or lemon juice, salt, cayenne, black and Jamaica pepper; put in, either cut down or whole, the head and feet; boil all together for an hour, and pour it into a deep dish. It is eaten cold with mustard and vinegar.'

To get the ball rolling, I decided to introduce some friends to a poshed up version made with pigs' cheeks, and perhaps owing more to that Italian way of serving meat, *agrodolce*, than the original recipe. Although a success, my 'rustic' presentation of the whole cheek, which sat quivering on the plate, caused some initial concerns. However, this is something a more talented chef than I will be able to address before it is unleashed on a paying public, so I would urge Heston or Marcus to give it a crack.

For pudding, naturally it had to be a spotted dog and custard. Alas, mine was only big enough to feed eight, and didn't require two men to transport it from the galley. And finally, as any O'Brian inspired feast should end, it was a toast in rum.

'To wives and sweethearts, may they never meet.'

F & K

Found Waiting
Mike Sim

They'll never be a 'Masterwaiter' on TV, I imagine. For two reasons. First, it would leave a fair amount of dyslexic teenagers rather disappointed on a Thursday evening; and secondly, while chefs are shown as passionate souls with fires burning deep in their belly, front of house staff appear damp, expunged of joy, with a complexion of damp granite.

For many, the art of waiting (and it is an art) is just a stopgap: a way to make ends meet whilst chiseling through education in the hope of making it out the other side clutching that all-important first class honours in synth keyboards and interpretive dance. But for others, whether through choice or necessity, it becomes their life, returning daily to the pass in a sadomasochistic bid for fulfilment, being screamed at incessantly, as, oddly enough, the gentleman on table four wasn't wholly satisfied with his still – frozen pea and ham soup.

These few will work their way through various establishments, all of which will leave them misanthropic and weatherbeaten by the storms of service. An endless whirlwind of emotion that'll toss them upside down, turn them inside out and crescendo with a thirty-seven pence tip, leaving their *papier-mâché* smiles cracked and sagging.

They'll return to the chain restaurant to serve the plethora of Pacmen shuffling the floor, mouths agape, waiting to be filled for under a fiver. They'll be at the beck and call of the hen parties guzzling booze like drag Vikings; they'll even smile politely when, after singlehandedly causing The Great Cava Drought of Britain, the customers decide it's best to split a sundae. Here they'll be stealth, an ambidextrous Vishnu, always there but never imposing. Especially not during the ten year anniversary dinner, because nothing says 'I love you' like an industrial-sized bottle of Lambrini and two for one on chicken fajitas (they're a lot like *fajitas*, only you pronounce the 'j').

Of course, after a while they'll need to spread their gravy-scented wings (oh

Icarus), and where better to do so than the great British Café? Here they can consume vast quantities of soup, during far more sociable hours, all the while wearing a fetching apron. It's a lot like a retirement home, only it smells more like moth balls and the customers aren't chained to the radiators. They will be required to master the craft of a *barista*, no mean feat, as coffee to caffeine addicts is like bait to anglers, carburettors to petrol heads or black pointy things to Goths: no matter how many colours, brands or sizes, their preference is the law. They must learn to apologise when, after making a coffee so breathtaking it would make the beatnik God himself weep, it is slandered as being not quite what the customer wanted, or worse, a little fancy, a feeling akin to spending days on an *impasto* mural, only to find out the client just wanted you to Pritt-stick micromachines to the wall.

As caffeine is to hipsters and intellectuals, alcohol is to wife beaters and broken nuptials. So it's off to the local pub, where they'll be treated just like one of the family – in other words, often undermined, frequently ridiculed and usually left helping someone off the toilet. It's not an entirely lost cause, however – who wouldn't want to know how to change a barrel of wine? Like Daniel in *The Karate Kid*, it will be an internship consumed with the mundane: polishing, tidying and occasionally sorting out the odd disagreement without using your fists.

On the customer service roller coaster, the local boozer is certainly the breaking point, the splintered curve that forces the server to question why they got on in the first place. But like the climax of the film (metaphorically speaking) they will stand triumphant, rising like a phoenix from the ashes, with a CV glowing brighter than an Essex girl's cheeks (the ones above the neck).

Yes – they will soar to the heights of fine dining, a dizzying climate thin with air but thick with cognac and fine wine. A utopia where vegetable oil has been replaced with glossy butter and the cutlery doesn't play *Teenage Mutant Ninja Turtles* with every bite. They will be Maître d, the St Peter of the catering industry, a deity in the front of house profession. Their word will finally be law; a quick nod and their staff will rearrange an entire room like an Acme tornado driving through a dusty western town. The customers will know them by name, and instead of screaming at them the chef now laughs with them over a glass of Bordeaux.

Through hard work, grit and determination they can go home at the end of their night knowing they've made it. They can look at their old apron and smile, they can relax knowing they don't have to try and bleach the smell of chip fat from their 99% polyester trousers. They can loosen their tie, take off their jacket, pour a glass of wine and revel in the rewards of catering stardom, thirty-seven pence richer. F&K

Photograph by Tom Gold
www.tomgold.co.uk

Stanley Green (1915-93) was one of London's best known eccentrics. From 1968 until his death, he patrolled Oxford Street six days a week, carrying a sandwich board and handing out hand-printed pamphlets. During his service in the Navy, he had been appalled by the lasciviousness of sailors, and formed the notion that too much protein in their diet was the cause. He devoted most of his life to passing this belief on to an uncaring public.

STANLEY GREEN

I rediscovered one of Green's pamphlets when researching small-press printing and realised that, though some of his ideas appear delusional, there's both humour and a kind of poetry in his expression of them.

Perhaps the most moving part of Green's mission is the way it is based not in a religious fundamentalism – he once told the *Sunday Times* that he prayed daily as '...a sort of acknowledgment of God, just in case there happens to be one' – but in what seems to be a genuine concern for the wellbeing of his fellow man.

Today, when it seems that everyone with a public platform wants to dictate to us what to eat for our own good, it feels a relief to remember someone who did it with such gentle innocence.

F & K

BEING DISCREET is an important part of respectability, and has assisted men and women to be virgins for their weddings, yet some had been to UNIVERSITY and other places of advanced learning, and had sexual friends at that time, and were very passionate, too. Being discreet helps to keep these people —faithful in marriage, as well. See page 4, line 21.

EIGHT PASSION PROTEINS WITH CARE

This booklet would benefit more, if it were read occasionally. And it deserves to be read at all changes of life: marriage, expectancy, menopause, retirement, old age, new situations, etc.

PROTEIN WISDOM

TOO MUCH protein and passion have afflicted humanity, with much distress and oppression.

Proteins are for body building; for body maintenance; and for reproduction involving the build up of passion for mating. Passion indicates a degree of readiness for mating, and is part of that readiness. Quite simply, protein makes passion. Most foods contain —some protein; but the eight passion-proteins are foods that have much protein, and that individuals eat frequently. So, how obvious it is that we should regulate passion, by regulating our eating of these eight classes of food.

The EIGHT passion-proteins are MEAT, FISH, and BIRD; CHEESE, EGGS; PEAS(incl. lentils), BEANS; and NUTS.

Those who do not have to work hard with their limbs, and those who are inclined to sit about —will STORE UP their protein for passion, during these spells of easiness. —Retirement could be a time of boosted passion and marital discord. —During prolonged extreme inactivity, one's needs of protein, could be very small.

MEAT, FISH, and BIRD, mean any creature of the land, or water, or air. —Fat is not protein. —There are many sorts of cheese, eggs, peas, beans, and nuts —all generally rich with protein. —Mostly, the proteins of plants lack the completeness of the proteins of creatures and of the proteins derived from creatures. Yet the lack of something might be very small, and another food would have a compensating abundance of it. So a varied diet could give enough of all the protein material needed for health.

1

Very passionate VEGETARIANS, note that five non-flesh foods are among the eight passion-proteins. —Synthetic meats of the future, will be rich in protein.

Advancing far into adulthood, we live more and more slowly, and married-love becomes harder to achieve, and so the cells of the body need less and less of protein. Elderly people are inclined to eat much more of protein than they need for health, so that some are stout; discontented and bad tempered: too passionate. Some old people could get their protein, mostly from milk, bread, potatoes(steamed), and other low-in -protein foods. Flesh foods and entrails are mostly coarse and fatty, and demand much DIGESTIVE EFFORT from aging constitutions.

At some time in our twenties, when the body comes to adult perfection and size, we cease to require protein for body building, and so passion gets a bonus of protein, if we do not eat less of protein, correspondingly. During late youth, energetic games would help to keep the passion gentle and help to develop the growing body, too. Yet, even a growing youth could eat more protein than the body required for health and development, and thus, by having strong passion, it might be very hard to be well behaved with a sexual friend, and to be headstrong in one's lonely bed: HARD to follow a responsible moral-code, in the unmarried years. —Use your unaided will, for as long as you can, to develop your character; but do not let passion defeat you, ALONE, nor with a sexual friend. These are important disciplines, in the still formative years.

Discipline in the single years, prepares us for the essential discipline of happy marriages. The fornicator becomes

married-love: ultimate physical-union; fornicator: single
2   person that partakes of ult. phys. union.

an adulterer too, because he was not taught to care, bringing unhappiness to others. —Some men have a child-like irresponsibility, and like cheats, they take mistresses, denying these women and their children the ASSURED PROTECTION AND CARE of a husband and father: deserting them when the thrills are finished.

PARTED spouses, AND PRISONERS should keep their passion gentle, in the meantime, for their contentment. And thus a lonely MOTHER would not be bad tempered with her children, while there were no married-love. —Husbands whose wives are 'expecting', should make their passion MORE and MORE gentle, until their wives are strong again, by having LESS and LESS of protein.

Some will not be lucky enough to marry, and others are conditioned AGAINST MARRIAGE; but they would find the essence of happiness, in having gentle passion all the time: free of fleshly longing, particularly at bed-time.

The REPRODUCTIVE SYSTEM is an extension of the SURVIVAL SYSTEM, and both systems function, in mating. The survival system works on and on; but the reproductive system rests for much of lifetime. The reproductive system could be permanently inactive; but the survival system would work on. The survival system has its needs of protein material, FIRST, and the reproductive system has the excess. For many people the surplus protein is always too excessive, making them too passionate, all the time. —If the survival system is disrepaired, or exhausted, the body is below MEAN-FITNESS, and the brain is distracted from mating-preparation, concentrating upon survival. In these circumstances, we do not develop passion for mating. When the bo-

3

dy comes again to the level of mean-fitness, then surplus protein builds up passion again. The mind is then inclined to be fascinated by sexual notions, and the more passionate we get, the faster the brain directs protein material to the reproductive system. —Mean-fitness is of an individual standard.

The reproductive system could become a parasite upon the survival system. For example, when a person's mean-fitness is sub-normal, and the body is building up passion and preparing for mating, while the survival system is still impoverished. It is conceivable that a person might be over addicted to fleshly pleasure, through years of weakness in the lonely bed. A spouse could be too fascinating, so that an environment of married-love could be taxing the other partner's strength, all the time. A husband might be anxious to keep an over passionate wife contented, with sufficient married-love, or anxious as some young men, to prove their worth as husbands. Such husbands might need to over exert themselves, so that other aspects of their lives should not be neglected, and through stimulants, might need to borrow strength that could not be repaid. Sometimes, both spouses look very weakened. Even a gentle person who stays long enough under the influence of sexual fascination BECOMES POWERLESS to resist it. Wives particularly, should not dress to seduce, too often. Single women: never.

Married-love is not for single people. And any kind of false married-love is shameful. Therefore, they should have only a GENTLE RISE AND FALL of passion. The will-power is usually defeated, in some way, by higher levels of passion. SPOUSES should be with their partners, when their passion is strong: avoiding temptation. —If married-love is

4

lacking, and death is only a generation of years away, and you are tempted to take a last fling, before you do any dishonourable lustful thing, do remember to be a good example to your grandchildren STILL.

Rarely, a little more lust might help a spouse. However, a spouse's natural capacity for married-love, might never equal the partner's, and the more passionate husband, or WIFE, usually would need to have LESS PASSION. —When we are regulating our proteins, we do not want more than is kind of married-love, and married bliss is secure, and without the burden of too much lust, our children are dear to us.

From the unhappiness that too much passion might bring, never escape into 'drinking'. Alcohol is a killer, and dulling the senses, it will not make you more pleasant to live with. LESS protein would moderate your passion, mend your marriage, and tend to restore health and affection to everyone involved. Contented people do not need to resort to drinking, smoking, and to other harmful, escapist pleasures.

LOVE-PLAY retards the husband, and hastens the wife, and in time, a wife too could reach the climaxes in married-love. However, a jaded wife is not likely to respond pleasantly to love-play, though she would permit married-love. A wife who is always jaded, so that the climaxes are not possible for her —will not sleep after married-love, and she is likely to suffer from ill health eventually. And be a poor mother, too. Married-love takes its toll of men as well. And for how many is it the last straw? —Do you find it hard to satisfy your husband, or is it an anxiety for YOUR HUSBAND to know how to keep YOU sweet, with enough married-love? —Mothers particularly, should remember that excessive passion is some-

5

times expressed, by smouldering bad temper towards the children too. Furthermore, when affection between the parents —has soured, home life is bitter for the children as well. Children need affection and tit-bits of adult wisdom, more than sweets and toys, to make them into UPright people: from BOTH parents.

BEWARE of the fun of indecent suggestions; of the amusement from the titillating scandal of private lives; of the diversion of the undress of low journalism etcetera. These things erode our morals and twist young minds.

Passion develops from that extra protein that we are not needing for health. Therefore, we should make ourselves quite gentle, for as long as we need to be. Later in life, the body loses its resilience for married-love; but even the spouse that fails FIRST, could be discontented and bad tempered, through eating too much protein. Both spouses should have less and less of protein, as married-love diminishes and old age advances, for life is 'running down'.

When the reproductive system becomes glutted with protein, further protein could turn to unwanted fat. In this condition, we would not have much to be smug about, and we might be dreadful people. —Bad temper, discontent, and violent outbursts, are some other ways of passion. We are keyed up, when we are passionate, TENSE, so that we have not only a heightened sense of fleshly pleasure, but also an increased sense of discomfort, to respond swiftly and aggressively against hurt and irritation. —People on high-in-protein diets, for remedial reasons, can utilize only a limited amount of protein, in this way, and the surplus will build up passion, perhaps excessively and UNHAPPILY. You can infer from this, that mean-fitness tends to assert itself again, and to adjust

6

itself sometimes, to extended disEASE.

Excessive married-love could bring physical or mental illness, to shorten life: an over-worked heart can not maintain effective nutrition to keep the body well.

The TENSION of passion will disorder our homes, our lives, and society generally. This tension will obstruct the rhythmical processes of the body, causing functional disease and debility. These things will be, if the SPELLS of gentleness and contentment between passion —are insufficient to keep us SOUND in mind and body. This tension makes us restless for distractions that destroy our health, too, like smoking, 'drinking', and drugging: three killers. The tension and restlessness of passion, if it be the burden of too much lust, could make us greedy, envious, and selfish people dragging at the bonds of family life, denying our children friendliness and conversation, compensating them, with dead things such as sweets and toys, pretending to be good parents, but thinking mostly of our own toys and pleasures and ease, as if having a family were no joy, and by being stern strangers to our children, we would fail to give them a decent moral code to live by. When such unwanted children have come to youth, they are often primed with a sort of foolish self-reliance, to make for themselves a world of fantasy and pleasure. They are without shame, or discretion, and unaware that moments of abandon could be fraught with many tears-to-come. When we are rid of this MANIA for proteins, there will be more, happy homes; fewer delinquent youths and fewer criminals; fewer psychopaths, fewer suicides; and not so many patients in hospitals. —Taking tranquilizers is foolish, when a LOWER LEVEL of PROTEINS could sedate you.

An individual's needs of protein are unique. ROUGHLY and GRADUALLY gauge yours. KINDNESS and PEACE

7

of MIND in you, would be pointers to how much you needed of passion and protein. —'Gentleness' is feeble passion, and is consistent with robustness; but feeling weak is quite different, and should be corrected, by less toil or a little more protein.

ENERGY is not passion. Sugars, starches, and fats, are the right foods for energy and warmth: never making passion. Nor will alcohol. Alcohol relaxes one's discretion, and FREES passion, at wrong times, in the MEANtime. —Some, might need more ENERGY for married-love. —If protein were being wrongly used to provide energy, because INsufficient energy-foods were being eaten, and then if sufficient energy-foods were eaten, THEN the amount-of-protein that had been MISused and that were still being eaten —would NOW be available to passion. Only APPARENTLY would the extra energy-foods be boosting passion; in fact, the formerly MISused amount-of-protein —would be the boost.

All living cells contain FATS being often pleasant to the palate, perhaps pleasanter than the PROTEIN of cells. And is not the popular sausage very rich with fat? And how little meat, it has! And herbs flavour it nicely, too. But, we may eat only judiciously of fat and oil, to make other foods nicer to the mouth. Then MORE would disorganize digestion.

Less protein would make some people thinner. Married-love keeps some men lean; but if they should put on some fat, by giving up some married-love, this would signify that they were now eating too much of sugars, starches, and fats, of ener-gy-foods. To stay thin, let them walk more; or eat less of these energy-foods.   *   *   *   *   *   *   *

Protein is the principal NON-WATER-SUBSTANCE in protoplasm, and PROTOPLASM is all the substance of bodily cells. Therefore, by regulating, day by day, the intake of

8   WEAKNESS could be caused by lack of ENERGY-foods.

protein foods, we can regulate the life of body cells, and this regulates passion.

MENOPAUSE: Its onset marks the LOSS of physical wholeness, and the individual needs less protein, permanently.

Protein Wisdom could assist with the Rhythm Method of family planning. A woman's PERSONAL MONTH depends largely upon the amount-of-protein that she eats, and upon the extent of her activity(in terms of the rate of the cell life of the body). The body is made up of developing and dying cells. —To adjust the personal month, more protein shortens the 'month', and less protein lengthens it. Similarly but contrariwise, more activity lengthens the personal month, and less activity shortens it.

A wife could make herself RHYTHMICAL in menstruation, by living to a pattern repeated every personal month. —Ordinarily, a wife lives to a weekly pattern, and this fits into the CALENDAR month; but her personal month is quite independent of the particular days of the week and of the calendar month: the beginning and the end of her cycle, falling on any day. —A personal month could have more, or less, Sundays than another 'month'; Mondays too; and so on. —If, for example, there were MORE Sundays in this personal month than in the next, and if Sunday were an idle, feasting day, for a wife on RHYTHM, then she would be eating more and be less active in this personal month than in her next one, if less food(principally protein) and more activity on another day —did not offset these irregularities. Thus this personal month would be shorter than her next one. What has been said of Sundays, applies to weekdays too.

In the rhythm method, a wife's schedules of work and of ease, should be SEVEN-DAY SCHEDULES: not weekly schedules. When her cycle came to an end, the seven-day schedules would re-start: on the first fully-menstrual day. Days of roughly equal exertion would be inter-changeable to implement the new personal month, because, for example, if this wife washed yesterday and her first fully-menstrual day were today, and washday were the first day of her schedule re-starting today, she could not have another washday today. During this 'month', her washday would fall on every SEVENTH day, and the substituting day(perhaps turning out a room) would fall on every FIRST day. Inter-changeable days could be MADE to balance each other: taking a little work off one, and putting it on the other. A diary and a plan of the days, would be helpful as a guide. —The SCHEDULE would ensure that each personal month had the same number of hard days, as another; the same number of easy days; off days; and so on. —About three or four seven-day schedules would make up each personal month. If a seven-day schedule were different from the others, because, for example, a day off were squeezed in, this would not matter, as long as this variation occurred in the same place, every personal month, and so formed part of the personal-monthly pattern. —Eating too would form part of this pattern: not gorging, just when tempted to do it. —Some tasks, like sending off father and the children, in the mornings, would have to fall into the schedule of the ORDINARY week, still.

A wife might be inclined to be more active, in the first half of her cycle; but this would not matter, if every personal month were the same, in this respect. —IDEALLY and perhaps naturally, married-love would form part of this personal-monthly pattern.

10

It is conceivable that a wife might learn to off-set una-voidable, irregular activity, by eating more protein. And like-wise, INactivity, by LESS protein. However, the 'FERTILE days' are enough to allow for some variation of rhythm; but being rhythmical is an advantage.

The HUSBAND, by regulating his eating of protein, could be gentle, during the fertile days; but he could be ready for married-love, as soon as the INfertile days came round. His wife being unable to adjust HER passion, would be very ready.　　*　　*　　*　　*　　*

For unusual exertion, the heart sometimes needs to be strengthened, by gradually increasing amounts of protein and exertion, first. Beware of habitual excess. —Rest, when you are tired: do not take a stimulant like tea. —Watch for chan-ges of season and work —that could alter your protein needs.

Animals kept from MUCH exercise, do not need much protein. Watch their tempers.　　—Some idea that you have hardly noted in this booklet, could be helpful to you, later. So keep it to read, again.

11

S O Green

Supplementary

SEXUAL ATMOSPHERE

Boy and girl companionships, co-education, love liter-ature-and-pictures, day dreams, and inactivity, from the start of sexual awareness, —TEND to bring early lust to youths, —with SICKLINESS and adult hazards. —The reproductive system must not be developed quickly, sacrificing HEALTH.

* * * * * * * * *

A young person with a personal month, might need to lengthen it, to have better health: by thinking—less of sexual-ity and by following lines 10-13, page 9.

It is important to marry, with good health.

Married people slowly killing themselves, with com-pulsive married-love, must lengthen the phases of recovery, by having healthy pursuits, away from thoughts of sexuality, and if necessary, by always having a lower level of protein.

Your excessive lust— could be fatal to your compuls-ive spouse.

ASSIMILATION: Strict vegetarians need complex meals to remake from digested protein, enough benign protein. 'When the re-making halts, between meals, for lack of particular material, the unus-ed protein-material becomes merely sugar for energy.' cf., p.1, last par.

CHILDREN and CONVERSATION.

Will your daughter be a —virgin, on her wedding? And your SON, on his? Or, are you out-of-touch with your children, and are some dirty minded school-children a much stronger influence upon your children than you, —conditioning them —to do shameful things a few years later?

When the novelty of having little children is over, and they want not to be cuddled so much, and the state reaches out to take our children, we begin to taste the old freedom of not having children about us. And if we have become very lustful, so that we are greedy and selfish, we shall resent the ties of our children and be glad for them not to seek our company. We shall be withdrawn from them, never talking to them as friends do, for the pleasure of it. The facility of conversing with our children, will never develop, and so we shall not pass-on to them our decent ways, nor our wisdom to bolster them later against the corrupting seductions of the media and 'arts', but firstly against the dirty talk of —children.

Be rid of excessive lust, to let kindness into home-life; to see beauty in our children; to wish not to have them defiled! Advise your children to walk away from dirty talk, and remind them of this discipline. This will allow you TIME for —gradually imparting to them your own decent, disciplined ways, through CONVERSATION, before they are corrupted.

And how many nice children are spoilt by parentless, DORMITORY years?

PROTEIN WISDOM (JUNE 1968),
34 HAYDOCK GREEN,   NORTHOLT,
MIDDX., UB5 4AR,   ENGLAND.
22nd.Variation.   36th.Thousand.
Price:11pence. Postage: extra. P.Orders to S O Green.

THE   COURTESANS

...and now the Prince— Royal up-bringing and royal parents are lacking, too—

We should be very concerned at the extent of sexual immorality, among students. Broadcasting, publishing, and acting, with their stock-in-trade of sexual arousal and intrigue— recruit from the colleges and academies.

Nor is the erosion of Marriage, merely by the matrixes of Fiction and Fun: a rag-bag BBC-group, seriously advised young people to 'experiment with sex'.

Young women that are intimate with men, will be denied marriage.

Nouvelle Cuisine ~ New New Cooking

Breil Bistro

'Food is fashion for fat people'

...said my friend, as we ate Malaysian noodles for lunch in West London. I was confused by her metaphor, then the words started to crystallise into a revelation. London does not have a true food culture yet, but is on an evolutionary journey which is currently closely following the rise of and glory of French cuisine.

London, like France, can trace its food culture evolution back to the individual's desire to be seen in the right or the best restaurants, and that individual's need to bolster his or her self-esteem with the belief that they know more than others about etiquette and food ritual.

We are in an *époque* that parallels the 1980s *nouvelle cuisine* movement in France. It has the same hallmarks: a desire from the public for something new; chefs with a desire for innovation; journalists (mainly bloggers these days) relentlessly pushing for change; the economic conditions required for innovation; and celebrity chefs being lauded.

It would be wrong to say that London does not have any food culture. It does. It is a culture of celebration of the instant discovery, belonging primarily to a small sub-group who require the latest, greatest and most hyped to satiate some primal need to be first and the best. We all need food.

Some of us love food. Some of us claim food and dining as a hobby. And some are moving beyond interest, into fashion, into fad, and even into fetish. The pinnacle of this food sub-culture are those who can predict the next food trends, such sage-like knowing elevating them above other mere food mortals.

That gratification and desire for knowledge and position also perpetuates the ever-growing secondary market: books, TV shows, pots, utensils and 'brand-celeb-chef' restaurants and supermarket ready meals. The chefs can be lured by celebrity and book deals (the appeal is hard to resist), but they must not forget their roots: they need to spend at least as much time in the kitchen as in Hollywood. Bocuse was the first to inspire great chefs away from kitchen and light the path towards publicity and infamy. Remaining in the kitchen in spite of the cause *célèbre* is necessary to preserve our culture and to mature it.

Exploration is a natural part and consequence of a growing food culture as we seek new foods, ideas and creations. In fact there is nothing new there at all. The London food culture must not end there; that cannot be its summit or its final resting place. In fact, we need to push beyond this fashionably fetish element of London's food culture. The culture needs to take its next evolutionary step so that we can learn to appreciate a restaurant for all that it is or should be: good food, cooked well, in a setting appropriate for the occasion (birthday, business lunch, informal meal), at the right price.

This next stage in our culture should see the breakdown of food snobbery and an embrace of all foods. The sneering must end and the over-hyped race to the next big blogger-filled, deity-chef-deigned, gastro-orgasm restaurant too. We can find solace in good food no matter where it is.

This is why we don't want to end up like the French whose cuisine has, over the past generations, waned in significance (whilst maintaining relevance to classic techniques). We should look, for example, to the Spanish, who prefer the reliability and heavenly cooked delights of the local place they're frequented for the past 15 years rather than boasting about the greatest new café in Catalonia — and this from one of the greatest discovering cultures in history: they discovered everything, and then realised the best was right at home. In fairness, the Spanish food renaissance is attributable to Spanish chefs pillaging *nouvelle cuisine* techniques and breathing Spanish life and interpretation into them. Even as Spain lights the culinary world at present, their food culture of local, reliable, regional and flavour remains steadfast.

Rather than have another culture do that to London's innovations and trends, London should mature and grow on what it has established so far.

London's continued ascendency is cause for celebration but not over-hype. London's challenge is to evolve internally and grow again to new culinary heights, and not get trapped in a downward decline spiral as the crowds move on, bored of more of the same. That requires us, the diners, also to mature and demand great restaurants with great ingredients at reasonable prices — the kind of place that we want to return to time and time again. Let's face it, it's London, we'll always have hype, but we need an establishment too that is the bedrock of a food culture beyond fish and chips.

London's food culture is currently fashion for fat people, or perhaps intellectualism for the English middle classes, who, like the French upper and middle classes, want to show their wealth, knowledge and prestige in society through food. Fashion and fad will always change, and that it should, because that's how we find new ideas. But those who've been around long enough will tell us that there is nothing new under the sun. So why not, instead, appreciate the wonderful restaurants that are hidden by the hype of the latest trend? Eat there instead, and if you like it, keep going back. *Allez!* F&K

BLOOD, STEW & HOO-DOO

RACHAEL BLYTH

How screwed up would your day be if you skipped your morning coffee fix?

Or if, heaven forbid, your butter-fingered spouse smashed your favourite mug?

What we eat is recognisably embedded in our social and cultural rituals. But it's possible that food is closely linked to more spiritual aspects of our lives too. The pomp and ceremony of roasting, grinding, brewing, inhaling and drinking coffee, for example, appears to have sprung straight from the pages of a fifth century grimoire. Its unique potency is akin to those wonderful sensory assassins that are usually found lined up in neatly labelled jars or, more often than not, stashed away in the far corner of a cupboard in suspicious-looking baggies. I can proudly say that as a teenager I attempted to smoke at least 50% of the substances displayed on my mother's spice rack, to absolutely no effect whatsoever. A great disappointment to my 13-year-old self, but the contents of the household spice store have intrigued and fascinated me ever since.

It is no coincidence that I am a one-pot kind of girl; I like nothing better than standing over the stove, wooden spoon in hand, tossing spices into my cauldron – sorry, pan – and hoping to witness some sort of gastronomical alchemy. That spices, like herbs, have been used to varying ends over the course of history very much adds to their intrigue and appeal. From the uses of cinnamon and myrrh in the embalming concoctions of the Egyptians, to the burning of rosemary and thyme in order to disguise the rancid stench of death in plagued environs, a strong whiff of mystique surrounds even the most commonplace spices.

The uses of such herbs in natural medicine is very well documented, from the asthma-relieving properties of sage to the anaesthetic effects of chilli. A cup of hot ginger is as certain to relieve indigestion as peppermint is to freshen the breath. Such treatments exist in all cultures across the world, even in 'sensible' Britain, where

Nicholas Culpeper's pioneering work has ensured an ongoing tradition of medical herbalism.

The fact that medical herbalism is derived from and was often a front for the more ambigious 'folk magic' of village cunning-folk is often overlooked in our sceptical and secular present. The mythology which surrounds each and every spice used in our daily dishes is rich and varied. Mint, for example, regarded as both breath freshener and (perhaps resultantly?) as an aphrodisiac, features in the tale of Pluto, who was reportedly seduced by the sweet perfume of the nymph Mente, much to the chagrin of his pomegranate-munching wife Persephone.

My love of one-pot wonders, my affinity with the mystical appeal of spices, draws me in particular to the African-American tradition of 'hoodoo' or 'conjure'. Like the glorious culture-mingling concoctions of gumbo and jambalaya, hoodoo stems from the diverse folk traditions of Africa, Native America and Europe. Unlike the complicated cults of Western esotericism, with their complex rites and clandestine rituals, the aim of hoodoo is to allow absolutely anyone to access supernatural forces in order to improve their day to day lives. Whether that means finding a tenner on the way to work or screwing over your irritating neighbour, hoodoo has a trick up its sleeve for you. Ok, so it's 'black magic' — it might occasionally entail injury to others — but it sounds fun, right? And unlike the neo-pagans we might find dancing in a trance around Stonehenge on the Summer Solstice, there is no charging or consecration of the ritual ingredients because the magic is already present, inherent in the roots and spices themselves.

This is a tradition which is intrinsically linked to food. The practice of adding spices, herbs and bodily fluids to food and drink is known in hoodoo-speak as 'laying a trick'. For example, to bind a new lover to your bosom you might, you know, drop a tablespoon of your menstrual blood into his spaghetti sauce. Such culinary wiles are referred to frequently in the music of the Delta Blues. In Dry Southern Blues, for example, Blind Lemon Jefferson disdainfully moans 'I can't drink my coffee and the woman won't make no tea/ I believe to my soul sweet mama gonna hoodoo me'. Likewise, Bessie Brown sings of her ingenious plan to get even with the woman who stole her man. 'Put a spider in her dumplin', make her crawl all over the floor'. Such eight-legged additions to the store cupboard were once prevalent in England too: in East Anglia during the 11th century it was common practice for very ill patients to eat live spiders wrapped in pastry. As the root doctor would say, don't knock it 'til you've tried it.

The use of spices in 'conjure bags' is still a practice common today. More than just lucky charms, such conjure bags have very specific purposes. Cardamom, a key ingredient in Ethiopian rituals of coffee making, is used in hoodoo as a tool for bringing about good luck in love and relationships. For example, one might chew cardamom in order to entice a potential mate at a social gathering. Rather conveniently, laying a trick will never affect those for whom they're not laid, so there will be no awkward mix-ups, just a whole lorra luck and lovin'.

Clove, known amongst medical herbalists for its fungicidal properties and an important 'warming' ingredient in Ayurvedic medicine, can be used to safeguard a vital friendship. If two people each wear red cord bags containing seven cloves until the cords break, they will remain firm friends for life. Clove is, in fact, remarkably versatile and can also be used to stop malicious gossip and lies, or when used in conjunction with cinnamon, to draw money towards the trick layer. One of my personal favourites, the humble caraway seed, doesn't just improve the flavour of root vegetables: it's also pretty good at warding off The Evil Eye.

Now all this might sound like a bag full of hocus pocus, a mish-mash of jiggery pokery and hokum. But the attribution of magical qualities to spices, particularly in Louisiana, a land where the primary ingredients (onion, bell pepper, celery) of regional dishes are proudly referred to as The Holy Trinity, imbues food with something of a spiritual purpose that I believe is not far off the mark. Less obesity epidemic and eating-disorder crisis, more appreciation for the multi-sensory healing properties of a slice of grandma's gingerbread, for the soul-soothing, organ warming effects of mulled wine or a glass of mead. Those cunning folk of the Deep South have already coined a catchy term for it. It's Soul Food. And we could all do with a bit more of that in our lives. **F&K**

COOKING UP CHARACTER.

Eleanore Johnson.

Saleem, the eccentric protagonist of Salman Rushdie's *Midnight's Children*, specializes in jams, chutneys and pickles. He believes he can preserve memory, history and mood within his famous preserves: a cook has the opportunity to infuse food with emotion. Those who eat Saleem's preparations ingest not only delicious food, but also some of the character and mood of the odd man who created the recipes. They absorb personality.

I love this idea.

As a one-time student of history, my cookery, though unaccomplished, is firmly anchored by an appreciation for food's wondrous capacity to conjure and encapsulate memory. I was reminded recently of Rushdie's Saleem proudly pickling history when, for my chef uncle's 50th birthday, my grandmother compiled a cookbook of all the family's favourite recipes. The project became a family collaboration and, as a tribute to the beauty and value of the final product, we have for some time been squabbling over the few copies printed.

My delight in the jealously coveted and already food-splattered copy I have so far managed to call my own is myriad. First and foremost, it is a gloriously versatile cookbook. It is also a wonderful lens through which to view the beloved grandmother who compiled it – a woman who, now 86, rivals Saleem in the character stakes. Fragments of her life and personality are divulged in the comments and photos she has included beneath each recipe. It is an undeniably South African product, revealing snippets of national and cultural identity, and, because of its progenitor's generation, a nostalgic whiff of colonialism. But most of all, these recipes – which read like stories – create a family history, told through the favourite foods of generations.

Although by no means chronological in association (the recipes are practically divided into food groupings), the cookbook yields a wealth of national insight. One recipe, for Snoek Bisque, recalls the

spice flair of Malay slaves in the Cape, and the 'good old days' when two shillings could buy a *kabeljou* the size of my young grandfather's calf, fresh from the harbour. A short Nut Soup recipe is followed by the rather longer story of its creator, a Miss Stella Bragg, who collected ostrich feathers to fund a trip to the Congo to see her fiancé – the aptly named Mr Diamond – where the natives asked her to undress because they were curious to determine whether white women were the same as black at bottom.

The potential cringe factor of these racially interesting anecdotes is assuaged by the guileless humour with which they are told. Nonetheless, with a typical post-apartheid sensitivity to anything that could be construed as racism, the youngsters in the family have always slightly dreaded the seemingly unavoidable taint of discrimination that infects our domestic history. Like the beautiful woman who gave my gran a memorable Chicken Marinade, some of our stories seem spoilt by a superiority complex.

Gran, however, cannot be accused of being backward. She tells of her insistence upon not wearing an apron when cooking, as a personal revolt against the position of women in post-war society. She also recalls a friend – whom we must thank for the Pickled Beef with Cherry Sauce – who got so hot cooking in a South African summer that she stripped down to only her apron. At the other extreme, Wheat Salad is associated with a winter so cold that the curtains were taken down to be used as extra blankets. (Why in this freezing weather Wheat Salad was popular remains a mystery.)

Other foods remind Gran of the giftless Christmases of the Depression years. And, substantially worse, the dry years when liquor laws meant no Wine Sauce could be made. But my favourite historically revealing anecdote comes with a Roast Venison recipe from Daisy Robertson. This woman's grandmother, along with other women from her farming community, took their children to live in hiding in nearby caves when Kitchener's scorched earth policy threatened their family homes during the South African War. They were eventually discovered and sent to a concentration camp but, thankfully, survived. The man responsible for betraying their hiding place to the British was given a farm as reward but received a rather humiliating comeuppance when, after the war, the women he had reported dragged him from his horse and grievously wounded him with their hat pins. This remarkable tale has come down the generations along with the venison recipe.

But apart from these more epic tales, this is above all a collection of family favourites, and therein lies its particular appeal. In her foreword my Gran describes the recipes as the stuff that has 'flavoured all our lives'. Many a recipe is accompanied by a photograph — weddings, *braais*, Christmas dinners, picnics, pets, homes. Many are attributed as somebody's particular favourite or have their origins tracked back to various ancestors or occasions. The Blushing Bride cocktail was made for an engagement party (although the bride

was not really the blushing type). Cheese Straws are associated, unappetizingly, with the cracked and bleeding feet of my uncle, who spent his childhood running barefoot around the dusty farm where he grew up. Hugh's Martini recipe was introduced to the family by the eponymous Hugh — a dental materials representative — who, no doubt encouraged by imbibing his own concoction, attempted to organize our distinctly unmusical family into a kitchen utensils orchestra.

There are many deaths and births, tears and laughter intertwined irrevocably with these simple and lovingly compiled recipes. It is wonderful to me that a Lemon Meringue Tart recipe that is only six lines long can encourage memories that fill pages; snatches of life framed by the food eaten by generations of family and friends. In a kind of synaesthesia of senses and soul, simple food proves far more than calories, energy or even pleasure; it is the stuff of culture and family. Food plays a weighty associative game with us. Just as Saleem pickles the years of his life into 31 jars of green chutney, bottling his experiences for others to taste, I am grateful that my family's appetites have now been packed into a cookbook. When I finally master these meals I will be feeding off more than meets the eye, or even the tastebuds. F&K

Snoek Bisque

250g smoked snoek, flaked (no bones!)
250g mushrooms, finely chopped
1 onion, chopped
2 tsps butter
30ml neutral cooking oil
50g flour
500ml milk
500ml chicken or fish stock
250ml sour cream
Juice of half a lemon
Salt and pepper to taste
2 tbsps chopped parsley, to serve

Sauté onion in butter and oil mix. Add mushrooms, sauté until onions are transparent. Stir in flour. Pour in heated milk and stock slowly, stirring until thick and smooth. Simmer 8-10 minutes. Add snoek. Heat – do not boil. Add squeeze of lemon juice and cream. Check seasoning, garnish with parsley and serve.

Best Before Dates

Josh Sutton

Best before dates were formally introduced during the 1970s, but some would say they have been around for much longer. They are a subjective entity, with a dangerous capacity to confuse the consumer. Ignore them, however, and your dinner party could turn to disaster.

Ostensibly designed to preserve our well-being, best before dates exist as an indicator; a subtle but never pinpoint clue as to when the ingredients within may be considered over the hill. Best before dates represent a point after which the constituent parts no longer gel. It's as though they have fallen out, or gone to seed. The harmonies have long since disappeared, leaving a foul taste rather than sweet music in the mouth. A best before date ignored could cause an embarrassment, a turned-up nose, and a painful wince that leaves you nostalgic for days gone by.

The current government is committed to ridding us of the potentially misleading information, albeit in a bid to save money rather than a genuine concern over a question of taste. New guidance published in the UK in September 2011 states that 'the best before date is a quality indication used by the manufacturer'. These new labelling guidelines, cited on the National Health Service website*, appear to take this a little further, and state that best before dates are more about quality, not safety.

*www.nhs.uk/Livewell/Goodfood/Pages/food-labelling-terms.aspx

I agree with this observation: it should always be about quality. But surely it is obvious that the consumer – rather than the manufacturer – is best qualified to determine both the validity of any date, as well as the degree of quality of the product itself?

The cynic may argue that best before dates are a mere con, a ruse, a tune conjured up by Mammon himself in a flimsily disguised effort to make us buy the latest version. An appropriate tool in this X Factor, disposable age of download avarice and instant gratification. Those of a more economical disposition claim that best before dates produce unnecessary waste, and it would seem that this school of thought has finally pricked the nation's conscience.

It's clear that best before dates are an indicator, rather than set in stone. A good helping of common sense as well as a keen sense of taste will ensure that your dinner guests don't desert you before pudding is served. For those of you who may doubt your own judgement, or are just a little unsure of these matters, I have devised my own best before framework. It's a simple indicator and a reasonably accurate tool, which will help dispel confusion, eradicate doubt and ensure that dinner guests remain firmly seated around your table:

AC/DC – best before *Back in Black*
Adam & the Ants – best before *Kings of the Wild Frontier*
David Bowie – best before *Scary Monsters (and Super Creeps)*
Echo & the Bunnymen – best before *Porcupine*
U2 – best before *The Joshua Tree*

You will in the end, have to make up your own mind, or be prepared to run the risk of disaster. It helps of course, if the food hasn't gone off as well. **F&K**

The Great Wine Ingredient Experiment
Mark Anstead

A man walks into a bookshop and to his great surprise finds it stocked geographically. Authors from Brighton, Edinburgh, London and Dublin fill the shelves marked 'UK' on the left, writers from America dominate the wall on the right, and a smaller 'Rest of the World' section is at the back.

'Excuse me,' says the confused man to a smiling shop assistant, 'I was looking for... crime?'

The analogy may sound far-fetched, but for many consumers that's what shopping for wine is like – extremely frustrating. Most retailers display wine by region, so we are first required to know the country of our ideal wine, which can be intimidating if you haven't a clue why an Australia Riesling is likely to taste any different from a German one.

The situation is just as bad in most restaurants. Why would I be any better off complementing my lamb with a wine made from grapes grown in the dirt of New Zealand than a similar wine from California? And how am I supposed to know?

It's no wonder many people simply follow half-price supermarket offers when buying wine. We are confused about the influence a local climate is supposed to have and particularly confused by France, which asks us to recognise a bewildering range of *châteaux* as easily if they were our local pubs.

So how do most of us, particularly if we are keen on drinking wine with home cooked food, approach wine? According to research conducted last year by Wine Intelligence, which monitors UK purchasing trends, grape variety is the number one factor in the minds of most consumers, closely followed by price promotions. Country of origin languishes in third place.

This should come as no surprise; knowing the grape is the easiest way to begin to predict flavours in a wine. Most of us know we are likely to taste blackcurrant in good quality Cabernet Sauvignon and buttery lemon, peach or passion fruit in a Chardonnay.

Wine is best enjoyed when drunk with food. It functions like an extra ingredient, adding a final flourish of flavours in the mouth to any eating experience. Get it right and it can change your habits forever.

Some wines are so acidic, for example, they demand vinaigrette on the salad. Others are so naturally herbal that adding too much thyme to a recipe will simply make them taste bland alongside it (best to leave the seasoning, in that case, to the wine).

Matching food and wine can be very subjective, but since the recession has forced many of us to entertain more at home the question of which wine pairs best with a certain dish bothers us more than ever. Being forced to buy wine categorised as a slice of a geography puzzle doesn't help.

Compare that confusion with a radically different approach being taken by a handful of wine shops in London. A few select retailers have taken to displaying wine by grape variety and now have sections in their shops devoted to, for example, Chardonnay, Riesling, Pinot Noir and Shiraz.

For food lovers, this could be a refreshing start to what we can only hope may become a trend. Ever since New World wines started to make a splash in the UK three decades ago, we have been learning about the tastes of the varieties they so helpfully list on their labels.

It's certainly more meaningful than expecting us to intuit a flavour distinction between 'France', 'America', 'Italy' and 'Spain'. (Although most of these retailers have cheated and kept country sections for Italy and Spain, because the grape varieties are obscure.)

In broad terms, then, this experiment should surely work, but the acid test is whether it actually increases sales. That is difficult to prove given the experiment is still in its early days.

There is only one thing for it: take a tour of some London shops adopting the 'wine by ingredient' approach (my words, not theirs) and see for myself how customers respond.

First stop is The Sampler in Islington, where white wines are displayed on the left and reds on the right. The main floor to ceiling categories for reds reads 'Merlot & Cabernet Sauvignon', 'Shiraz' and 'Pinot Noir', and there are single shelves devoted to less popular grapes such as Malbec and Mourvèdre.

After a few minutes looking around, I notice Laura, a pretty 29-year-old interior design student at Sheffield Hallam University, and I chat with her to see what she feels about the way the shop presents its wines. I quickly discover we share a common interest in food.

Laura's wealthy (sounds-like-an-entrepreneur) boyfriend frequently drives her down to London in his BMW so they can spend time with his best mate. The picture I begin to get is that he and his friend love these weekend jaunts, if for no other reason than Laura seems willing to do all the cooking.

'The first thing on my mind when I shop for wine is to buy something to go with the dish I'm preparing,' she says. 'And I find it far easier in The Sampler than any wine shop in the North.

'Laying wine out this way instantly helps me focus. I know I don't like Chardonnay so I don't waste time in that section, but if I fancy a citrusy Sauvignon Blanc I can find it easily.

'I don't know much about wine, but I know what I like and I love coming here whenever I am in London. I've even thought I might one day open a shop like it up north – it's such a good idea.'

I should add that there is another advantage luring shoppers like Laura into The Sampler: 25 bottles loaded into machines around the shop dispensing small tastings if you are willing to shell out a portion of the retail price. On a £15 wine,

for example, you can pour a 25ml tasting for around 70p.

The Sampler has two branches in London, but it isn't the only retailer abandoning the geographic approach. When Oddbins collapsed into administration last year the news made national headlines, but a new investor bought 37 stores and re-launched them, giving managers the choice of how they would like to stock and display.

Two Oddbins shops in London decided to shelve mainly by grape and as soon as I walk into the West Hampstead branch I am greeted by what is now a familiar sight. Here the white wines are listed under 'Chardonnay', 'Sauvignon Blanc' and 'Riesling', with smaller shelves dedicated to less popular grapes such as Viognier and Gewürztraminer.

There are no tasting machines to lure customers, and the shop has only been selling wine this way for three months, but manager James Hatherley believes the new approach helps educate his customers.

'If I had a pound for every time someone told me they don't like Chardonnay but quite like Chablis I'd be rich by now,' he laughs. 'Many people don't realise Chablis is Chardonnay, but when they see them stocked together in one section they begin to understand. It gradually demystifies French labels for them.'

Old habits die hard, though. While I'm standing chatting to James a middle-aged woman wanders into the shop and seems slightly confused. Eventually she announces she is looking for a

Côtes du Rhône. James directs her to the section marked 'Shiraz' and indicates the Côtes du Rhône bottles. The woman's eyes scan the shelves trying to work out the association between this and Australian Shiraz, so we talk for a few minutes and I conclude she was actually seeking 'Côtes du Rhône' mainly as a brand – something she has picked up as fashionable among her friends.

I'm even more surprised when a younger woman, apparently a regular customer, picks up a bottle of Pinot Noir and tells me she hadn't even noticed that the shop was laid out by grape.

'I just come in here and ask for suggestions,' she says, looking at me blankly. Then she scans the store again and her eyes widen in realisation.

'Oh yes, I see what you mean now,' she giggles. 'I thought something had changed in here since last year, but I couldn't put my finger on what it was.'

What this demonstrates is how many consumers still need help choosing wine. Thankfully a local independent wine merchant has a lot to offer over supermarkets (where advice is thin on the ground).

The last stop on my tour is The Theatre of Wine in Tufnell Park where customer assistance has become essential. Here I am really confused – there are no headings over shelves (neither by region nor grape) and when I spot a New Zealand Pinot Noir sat next to a Gamay (Beaujolais) I begin to suspect the shop has been arranged by some secret code.

'We display by style – light-bodied nearest the front moving to full-bodied at the back,' explains manager Jason Millar. This explanation turns my brain upside down, so I ask him to talk me through it.

'It means customers need more help from us,' admits Jason, 'and we usually start by asking what kind of wine they like. A lot of people either say 'light and refreshing' or 'full and rich', so then we immediately take them to the correct part of the shop for that.

'More than a third of customers mention food – they want to pair a wine with what they are cooking. If it's fish, for example, then you want something light-bodied that won't overpower the delicate flavours, but it needn't necessarily be white.'

After half an hour talking to Jason, I begin to feel at home with shelving by style, and I can see the advantages to staff as they guide customers. But making it essential to have a conversation before every purchase seems risky. Jason assures me it works, at least in Tufnell Park.

I return home to Essex feeling a little envious of Londoners and the handful of shops I have found prepared to break so radically with tradition. It must work or they would surely abandon the experiment, but the wine industry is slow to change and new ideas are never embraced quickly.

My thoughts turn to my own choice of wine for the evening. I'm eating fish with a smoked mozzarella sauce, so a lovely slice of oaky, buttery Chardonnay would do the trick. From Australia? France? California? Oh, who gives a monkey's – just gimme that wine. **F&K**

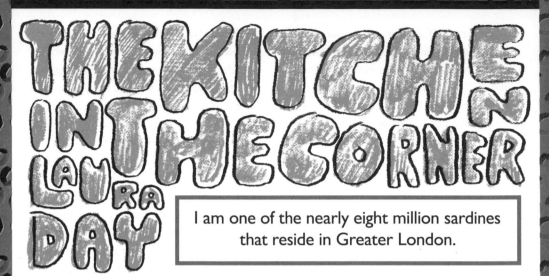

THE KITCHEN IN THE CORNER

LAURA DAY

> I am one of the nearly eight million sardines that reside in Greater London.

I live in a rented studio flat where my bedroom is my kitchen. I can roll out of bed and into my shower in less than three complete moves. Having upped sticks from a much larger chunk of available cooking area in Australia (a country known for its vast expanses) it may come as no surprise that I've spent the past 18 months of my life here sussing out the best way to use the virtually non-existent space that, under duress, I refer to as 'the kitchen'.

Firstly, there was an epic compromise on the lack of storage. Having just three cupboards above the sink and no drawers at all, the early days weren't too bad, given I didn't own so much as a teaspoon. But as I clanked home, weighed down with plates, pans, cutlery and mugs after an extensive shopping trip, it dawned on me that no, my kitchen cupboards aren't an incarnation of the TARDIS and that I didn't, in fact, have anywhere to put my food. I metaphorically boxed away my love of found retro bakeware

and serving platters emulating the glossy spreads of my cookbook collection, and began applying the Tetris skills I'd perfected during childhood to piling up the cupboards.

While the next few weeks were spent in a constant state of rearrangement, they were also open to waves of impulse disposal, accidental smashing and occasional crying. Things had to change.

I spent roughly six months waging an ugly war between the pans and the pantry, swapping plates for pasta and rehousing them in the much harder to reach area above the extraction hood. This rearrangement lasted for the duration of exactly one meal's preparation before I swapped everything back.

I had, somehow, to extend the kitchen. And so began the search for kitchen space savers, where I dreamed of a chrome contraption adorned with at least four hooks and which was strictly no nails. I trawled storage websites to no avail. I palpitated at the thought of DIY. After several unsuccessful searches (with some desperate midnight Googles through bathroom caddies), I finally found it. Like a knight in shining armour ready to take me into its perfectly welded arms, this particular find was a holy grail of six hooks and would hang like a shrine to all things storage on the back of my front door. It would serve me as a mug tree pot hanger utensil stacker, with space even for the box grater. I bought two.

I boxed up my spices and proudly moved them into the newly-freed up pantry space: two whole cupboards! There is a top shelf of casserole dishes, ramekins, mixing bowls and glasses, and a bottom shelf of spices, pastas, pulses, condiments and the cutlery caddy. I'd also wised up to the once overlooked top of the cupboards and upgraded it to pride of place for those non-essential and yet vital bits and pieces: porridge oats, icing sugar, cupcake cases, a lifetime supply of no-sodium baking powder. They are just a dining chair, a hazardous stretch and a hernia away from being in my easy cooking reach.

Despite more or less sorting the storage issue, there remains a fact that no amount of shiny hanging chrome can improve, and that is the worktop. Using this kitchen for its original intention is tricky, owing to a literal three-piece setup of a sink, a square of worktop and a hob. The worktop space where the magic is supposed to happen is shared with a knife block and what now seems like an oversized joke kettle. My ever-growing enthusiasm for cooking often looks like it will swell beyond the means of my abode, when I find I've run out of room as soon as I get my ingredients out. But with a swift karate blow to the throat of how I lived in my student days, I decided that cleaning-as-you-go and multitasking was the way to go, if only to avoid slipping into the abyss that is chopping veg in the sink.

When the need for a blender was realised, it could only be in micro form. Yet it's the perfect size for curry pastes and batch blending, and I now whizz away with room to spare for the chopping board. I tidy as I go and do the washing up if crockery Jenga begins in the sink. Pastry rolling and bread making can often stray into the moderately difficult, and usually sees the knife block being relegated to the floor so I can get the perfect 2.5cm pastry. Special dinners require planning: nothing unusual there, you might say, but where your usual domesticated dweller may shimmy around a kitchen of plural work surfaces as one course sets and another bubbles away, I've become accustomed to advanced prepping, IKEA-esque organisation and time management fit for the boardroom.

While I've quite probably developed a mutant strain of OCD as a result of these quarters, it does have a point to prove. No, you don't have to use your oven for storage or resort to reheatable dinners. And yes, you can bake your own bread and cook a three-course meal in the same night. It has shaped my efforts in cooking, making me face any dish that requires two knives and several pots head on. I've refused to let our once rocky relationship make me feel I can't make it work. And so for richer for poorer, for better or worse, till lease us do part, my tiny kitchen and I are, for the moment, quite perfect. **F&K**

Rendezvous at a Steakhouse in Melbourne by Zoh.

They were only going to have coffee.

Not even food. Just coffee. Sue and Ren had been Facebooking each other tirelessly for 12 months.

Sue was a keen food photographer and freelanced for various magazines and projects that generally had a green focus. Pictures of scrumptious organic goat feta crumbled over soft-boiled eggs and hand torn pieces of free roaming chicken breast on top of a pile of fluorescent green Japanese seaweed salad or things of the sort constantly popped up on Ren's newsfeed. Sue was creative, humble and loved hearing what people thought of her work. Ren found that incredibly attractive and strangely sensual,

for he loved food and loved saving the planet one small step at a time.

In fact, Ren and his Japanese mother made the seaweeds in those photographs. They ran a little organic shop in Kamakura, a city 50 kilometres south of Tokyo. That batch of seaweed was one of the first they had mailed to Australia during the Japanese winter, when no-one wanted to tuck into a cold salad like that. Obviously the chefs at the restaurant had added additional ingredients to the seaweed. Vinegar and brown sugar by the look of it, and maybe just a tiny bit of soy sauce. Ren was fine with that. He thought his seaweeds looked happy, soaking in a pool of responsibly produced sauces with the hot Melbourne sun visible in the background. 'Ah, my seaweeds have gone on a summer holiday,' thought Ren, with a contented smile.

Sue put up two photos of a juicy wagyu mini burger tasting platter, accompanied by local beer sweating in a schooner. Ren could almost feel the cold beads of water clinging to the glass with his finger tips. 'It's two degrees here, Sue. Thanks for bringing a bit of sunshine to Kamakura!' Looking at her photos from Melbourne, Ren felt warmer inside.

Sue always liked Ren's comments. Japanese food was big in Melbourne, and to have the maker of those sweet sticky seaweeds following her photographic career had been quite special, she thought. Could you imagine anyone you knew making those seaweeds at home? Sue had once sat through a documentary, on the equivalent of the Discovery Channel for Japanese food shows, on how those seaweeds were harvested. She was dumbfounded. They showed men swathed in full protective rain suits and life jackets crowded on a boat bobbing furiously in the open sea. It was completely dark but for the spotlight enveloping the men struggling to haul up an enormous pile of dark brown seaweed plants from the foaming water. Sue thought the plant looked like Chinese black fungus. The humungous flaps of seaweed were processed immediately; she could not believe her eyes when the dark brown seaweed swiftly turned sharp fluorescent green under heat. She'd always thought some sort of food colouring had been involved, but no: it's like magic. Like pooris and loukoumades puffing up in hot oil. Irreversible, instantaneous, deeply satisfying.

She'd never asked Ren about how he made the seaweed. Was it as magical as what she'd seen on TV? She's afraid Ren might give her a noncommital smile and tell her that it's all a hoax, sensationalised for impressionable TV viewers like her. It's one of her favourite trivial factoid TV moment which she recounts endlessly to her friends and family. And strangers as well. Not many people knew or cared enough to find out how the seaweed came about. It's just there, neatly packed by invisible hands into little plastic boxes. But Sue cared. She cared a lot about what she knew to be interesting facts. She wanted Ren to agree, and only agree with her.

Ren asked about the waygu burgers. He hadn't had much meat for some time, he said, on the instruction of a wise man in the community who recommended a diet low in meat (beef in particular) to strengthen Ren's daily prayer at the temple for Ren's mother, who'd been sick for too long. 'I practically live on seaweeds, tofu and vegetables now. It's not that bad!' chimed Ren, though Sue knew that Ren loved beef. He had once had Australian beef at a posh restaurant in Tokyo, when he and his mother were celebrating the expansion of their business to Australia and New Zealand. They were happy, grateful and mused over the coincidental presence of the delicious slab of medium rare Australian steak. Pink like a girl's blushing cheeks in the dim light.

Business or leisure? Frowning, Ren was not sure which box to tick on his Incoming Passenger card. After his mother died, Ren just had to get away, and their growing business in Melbourne needed help. Stepping into the dry heat, Ren realized it had been exactly one year since his first box of seaweed had arrived here. Sue was one of the first food photographers to document the beginning of his now burgeoning career. Her photographs made it feel real. His seaweed really had made it across the continents and the vast oceans. Somewhere outside Japan. Somewhere he'd never been before. He had the photo framed and it stood on top of the humble glass display cabinet in his Kamakura shop. There had been many more pictures taken by photographers like Sue, but Ren only kept that first photograph he found on Facebook. He didn't really know why.

At the airport, Sue with her orange hair in a ponytail and wide-framed sun glasses pushed on top of her head was extending her hand and beaming at Ren. It was Ren who first recognized Sue, as she really did stand out in the crowd with her shock of orange hair and bangs cut straight across in a neat line just above her eyelids. 'Konnichiwa!' she said. Sue had learnt Japanese in high school and could still remember the basics. Ren was suddenly filled with excitement. For a moment he was deflected from his silent commemorating of his late mother, whom he had always pictured next to him on his maiden voyage to Australia.

They talked and talked, and exchanged first impressions of each other based on their Facebook accounts. Ren had seen Sue's infectious smile and daintily painted red lips on her profile, but he himself had been too shy and absorbed in his business. His picture had always been that of the various seaweeds in season. Besides, Sue had never asked to see a photo of him. He smiled at Sue who as always seemed to be radiating happiness. 'Hey, how about we go to the new café on

Bourke St? Or we could go get something to eat if you're hungry?' asked Sue. He was the seaweed man! He's here and he's my guest of honour! Secretly, Sue made up and hummed a little song about Ren in her head.

Neither of them was hungry, so they agreed to a taste of the best coffee in Melbourne's central business district. Ren marveled at the beautiful coffee art and the creamy foam before gingerly sipping his latte. He was slightly drunk on what was happening around him and started to feel more relaxed. Sue was a lot warmer in person than he thought. He had been surprised at her offer to show him around Melbourne. And to pick him up from the airport too.

Sue was wearing her sunglasses now. Ren stared absent-mindedly at his reflections on the lenses. Two of him, identical but not the same. Sue looked down into her cup of cappuccino and smiled at him mischievously. How tempted she was to ask him how his seaweeds were made. The question had been gnawing at her for the past 12 months, and yet she had let the opportunity pass. Ren sensed there was something on Sue's mind. It was a novel feeling; over the internet he simply was not able to have sensations like that. Like beautiful photographs of food that had no smell or taste.

Ren opened his wallet and took out a small photograph of his mother taken on a walk down the Pacific Ocean coast where the seaweeds were sometimes collected. He had changed since his mother passed away. He had had to. Looking at Ren, deep in thought, Sue asked 'What do you remember most about your mother? She seemed like a nice person.' Ren cocked his head slightly and smiled. 'Funny enough, it would have been that glorious piece of Australian steak we had in Tokyo. We were on top of the world.' Before they knew it, they were on their way, catching the first of two trams that would take them to a small family-run steakhouse, off the beaten track but well known amongst Melbournians.

Sitting across from Sue at a small table by the window, Ren raised his wine glass and looked at Sue through the glass. The aroma of the shiraz was complex and intoxicating. He relaxed into the cushy chair. 'Your eyes are just one shade darker than the seaweed in the very first photograph you took of that organic chicken dish. Do you know that?' asked Ren. 'Sue, have you ever wondered how seaweeds were made? Most people don't really care one way or the other,' sighed Ren.

'I'm listening.' said Sue. F&K

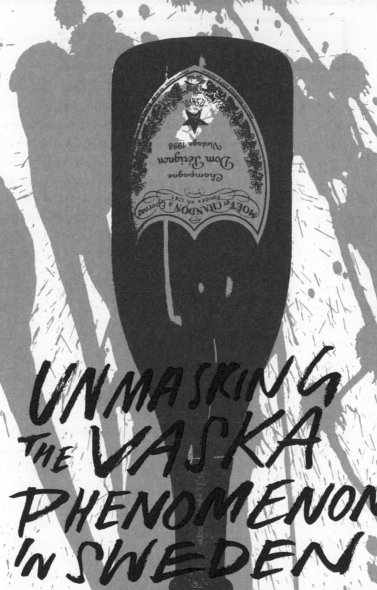

UNMASKING THE VASKA PHENOMENON IN SWEDEN

JONATHAN BROWN

Swedish food culture is a hot trend right now.

It acts as a virtuous, refined, stripped back counterpoint to the excesses we've seen in Western culture in recent years. Where we once loved rich sauces, bling ingredients and status, we now hanker after local, foraged, fresh and ethical culinary experiences that the likes of Fäviken deliver by the basket load.

And it's even less of a surprise that Swedish culture is blazing a trail too, in the guise of Larson's *Millennium Trilogy*, Nudie Jeans, Acne and Wallander, as they offer a very human and egalitarian return to human first principles. There's nothing showy, frilly or decorated about these artifacts, and that textured simplicity is what attracts us to them in a time of recession-induced cultural reappraisal.

It all ties into a social theory called *lagom* which pervades Swedish culture. *Lagom* as a word has no direct translation. But, as ever, where you find such slippery words, you often find the key to understanding that culture. *Lagom* means, broadly, 'to act in a balanced, moderate and reasonable way'. *Lagom* is the bowl of porridge in *Goldilocks and the Three Bears* that is just the right temperature.

This sense of balance is most noticeable when you work with Swedes, who knuckle down solidly from nine till five, then clock off *en masse* and head home to their families as a way of maintaining a balanced life where family comes way before work. *Lagom* also set the conditions for fashion to have been almost literally banned in Sweden for the decades following WWII. It was seen as being too showy to wear branded clothes, let alone anything from the designers of Paris or Milan, or even to wear anything that made you stand out. So bright colours and daring new cuts of cloth rarely saw the light of day. Only in the 80s did fashion courses spring up and fashion columns emerge in newspapers.

Whilst this exhibitionist austerity has clearly abated, with the recent rise of H&M, you also glimpse the relics of this historical constraint exhibited within the upper echelons of Swedish fashion. Jackets often have impeccable detailing in areas that no-one will ever see; shirts have elaborate needlework behind collars and cuffs; and a trend has arisen for Happy Socks which allow Swedes to express themselves by flashing a bit of eccentric colour from the ankle every now and again. With all of these examples of hidden self-expression, only those in the know understand the hidden cultural code.

We've grown to admire Sweden's *lagom*-driven discernment and refined aesthetic, as their chefs and creative leaders have set the cultural agenda in Europe recently. But what I suspect you haven't heard about is the barbaric flip side of this good taste. Because for every cultural movement there is an opposite, but not always equal, reaction. And in Sweden, this reaction is the phenomenon of *vaska*.

To *vaska* literally means to pour away. It apparently started in the Stureplan district of Stockholm and at the annual tennis tournament in Båstad during the early 2000s where the brat pack gathered each year – effectively Sweden's answer to Sloane Rangers descending on The Cartier Polo or tottering around with treasure chests in Mahiki. They would order the most expensive champagne, often in enormous bottles, and spray it all over the bar like a Formula 1 driver. The bars and clubs banned this spraying, so instead the brats would ask for two bottles of champagne and would ask the barman to *vaska* (pour away) one of the bottles down the sink. For some it was a mark of honour to not be noticed whilst *vaskning*, but was instead something to brag about with your friends.

If you visit www.funistrada.com/vaska, I've gathered up a collection of YouTube clips which show people *vaskning*. My favourite shows a 20-something-year-old dancing like a peacock whilst a gigantic bottle of champagne is carried by two waiters on their shoulders before being ceremonially poured on the floor.

This trend was so anti-*lagom* that it was explored in 2002 in a Swedish documentary called *Young and Rich in Sweden*, which portrayed a gauche and arrogant collection of *nouveau riche* Swedes who loved the limelight that made most of their compatriots feel sick at the thought of such brash behaviour.

This exposure only fuelled the phenomenon. A website emerged called www.smsvaska.se that let people deduct money from their bank account for nothing in return, except the feeling of smugness you get from wasting cash; pop songs were released of singers making fun of the trend with a spoof bling rap video (http://svtplay.se/v/2157987/kakan_och_julia_champagne-vaskning); and I've heard from Swedish friends of people going to Michelin-starred restaurants and ordering two tasting menus for themselves, to then eat just one dish per course and send the other back untouched, with the instruction that the waiter should throw the other dish away. God only knows what the chef thought of the situation.

More recently the *vaska* trend has evolved into *traska*, which means 'to trudge away'. Another Swedish friend told me of a rumour that a man had insisted on paying for his very expensive dinner in advance only to then walk away and leave it all behind. And *Aftonbladet* (Sweden's equivalent of the

Sun) ran an article about a man who paid for 50 hamburgers from a fast food restaurant, ate one and then walked out, having dumped the other 49 in the bin. With all of these examples it's unclear when, where and how often it happens, because part of the pattern is to do it quite discreetly: a warped sort of *lagom* approach to behaving in an anti-*lagom* way.

But the key question is why it happens at all, especially as it is so out of keeping for Swedish culture. And precisely in that contrast resides the answer. These people are behaving wastefully as a way of showing off and gaining attention in a land where fitting in, being moderate and keeping yourself to yourself is the well-studied norm. It's two fingers up to good taste, a declaration of wealth and an act of rebellion against Swedish conformity.

Part of the answer also lies in politics. In spite of our warm view of Sweden as egalitarian and rational, it is, in fact, one of the most snobbish societies in the world, with rich industrialists and conservative views abounding. The Swedish Sloane Rangers who are driving this trend are probably part of the *överklass*, or posh élite, who have gained a cultural foothold as the *socialdemokraterna*, the Social Democrats – the more working class party – have lost their hegemony. Or more likely, they aren't quite part of this élite group, but wish they were, so are acting in a debauched way to prove themselves. It's interesting that as the Social Democrats have lost political control, so too the previously untouchable nature of *lagom* has begun to be questioned, with phenomena such as *vaskning* being a niche case in point.

Clearly brattish behaviour is not restricted to the nouveau posh bars of Sweden – Yuppies have been showing off their wealth all over the world since money was invented. But it is the righteous indignation from *lagom*-minded Social Democratic Swedes that this has precipitated that makes this trend even more curious. For instance, one article in *Aftonbladet* about *vaskning* was swamped with 172 comments, which ranged from the dismissive to the psychopathically outraged.

When I mention this phenomenon to Swedish friends, they normally become quite uncomfortable. Some even deny that it exists, or say that it was just a fad. But often they go on to say they've heard a rumour of another act of *traskning* depravity. They feel embarrassed by this obnoxious behaviour and want to distance themselves from it. It just goes to show that it's often the outliers and liminal artifacts in culture that shed the most light on how a society ticks. At a time when the 99% Occupy Campaign is all over Europe and America, the *vaska* and *traska* trend, whilst niche, class-driven and elusive, just make Sweden's *lagom* culture even more of a cultural lighthouse. **F&K**

The Gourmet Sublime — Jessica Keath

Plato once said that those who seek knowledge are clinging to a recollection of something they once saw.

I don't pretend to know anything much about Plato, but I do know that I am clinging to a recollection of something I once ate: a lunch that has left me tetchy and whiny in the face of all subsequent meals. I was 14 when this benign epiphany arose, calmly, from a set of circumstances so odd as to warrant my sad conviction that it will never happen again.

I had been working at Russell's Pizza, a culinary institution set in an old (by Australian standards) Cornish cottage on Willunga High Street. Open for just one night a week, its credentials weren't based so much on its excellent pizza, as on the experience. This was afforded in large part by the magnanimous character of the restaurateur himself. While one could look forward to a very fine yoghurt panna cotta at the meal's end, one would be equally within one's rights to expect a ponderous conversation about serendipity or theories of war, or both. Known by the local women as 'Russell the love muscle', he

spent many an evening deflecting their drunken affections. He was short of leg but well endowed with charisma. It was no doubt with these libidinous women in mind that Russell agreed to an Argentine gentleman holding tango classes in his ballroom.

This ballroom, it must be said, was one of the finer contributions Willunga made to the modern world. From the outside it was a humble though not entirely graceless corrugated iron shed. Inside, its polished concrete floor (dusted with lime powder) was large enough to house the massing tango aficionados, but small enough to enable an opportune grope.

Exactly why this hot-blooded dance form took off in the uniformly white pseudo-gentry of a small country town remains unknown. Some cite the local lack of amenity, others the teacher's wavy black hair, though it is commonly agreed that menopause had something to do with it. The dance floor showcased a selection of not yet expired male virility and last ditch female passion – pairs of sweaty palms aiming for a neat 'three minute marriage'. The release of Sally Potter's self-directed, self-starring and self-aggrandizing film *The Tango Lesson*, promising sexual reawakening, only inflamed the situation. Joining them on occasion was a clump of mildly precocious teenagers, who were deemed too young to practice such a prurient dance. These concerns were defunct on my part, as I stomped my way across the ballroom in my Dunlop Volleys, artlessly ignoring any basic rules of seduction.

Though my kinaesthetic talent called for further tutelage, I was adept at weighing out 120 grams of pizza dough by feel. Working amid the smell of the wood-fired oven in a flour-covered apron with a coworker calling orders promoted the sense that all was right in the world, bar the odd hiccup. The open layout of the unorthodox kitchen saw me chatting rather too much with customers, and I will never again forget to add yeast to the dough. Among the pizzas on offer were some standard favorites: Supreme and Seafood — the point of difference being the exhibition of whole oyster shells and the occasional unadorned leg of crab. Also on the menu in addition to these staples were examples of Australia's genuinely cosmopolitan cuisine: Turkish lamb pizza, dukkah with olive oil, halloumi, pavlova. The seamless extension of eccentricity from kitchen to table was best evident when Russell's 11-year-old son offered to lend a hand on the floor one evening. Upon clearing a dessert and being told, 'Sorry, I'm not finished,' he waited chivalrously as the astonished customer finished her final mouthful from the plate in his hand. Needless to say customers had no choice but to be charmed, lest they be found guilty of 'not getting it'.

And so it transpired that I came to be loitering at Russell's when the tango teacher (let's call him Eduardo) popped by for an impromptu lunch. He was quiet and manly. He had that very un-Australian ability to wear chinos well. He could guide one from A to B in an expeditious yet salacious manner that belied one's own clumsiness. I liked him. After a round of the floor with some tango faithfuls and a glorious three minutes with me, Eduardo joined us at a set of wooden tables arranged in the courtyard under the grapevines. I was astounded that such attractive and civilized people could assemble around equally attractive food. The sensuality that had eluded me on the dance floor presented itself with charm and ease amid the local kalamatas and the anchovy pizza. I still believe that Willunga olive oil with bread and dukkah cannot be trumped. (This was before dukkah graduated to a sawdust-aping staple of the *petit bourgeois* 'gourmet' supermarket. Russell's was made with love and care and a type of preindustrial grinder.)

It would be trite to ascribe the meal's brilliance to its simplicity, so I hereby declare myself a charlatan and say the cliché is so. Don't get me wrong — I love a 16-hour sous-vide squab neck in heat resistant *cèpe* jelly amid a lecithin laced, gravity defying pea *velouté* as much as the next person, but this peasant meal wins. The combination of sunshine, Eduardo and the wine sent me into such an ecstasy that I have since remembered that day with a quasi-mystical reverence. The Sublime is said to be that which is ineffable, that which cannot be put into words. Some experience it in the face of mountains; I experienced it at lunch. **F & K**

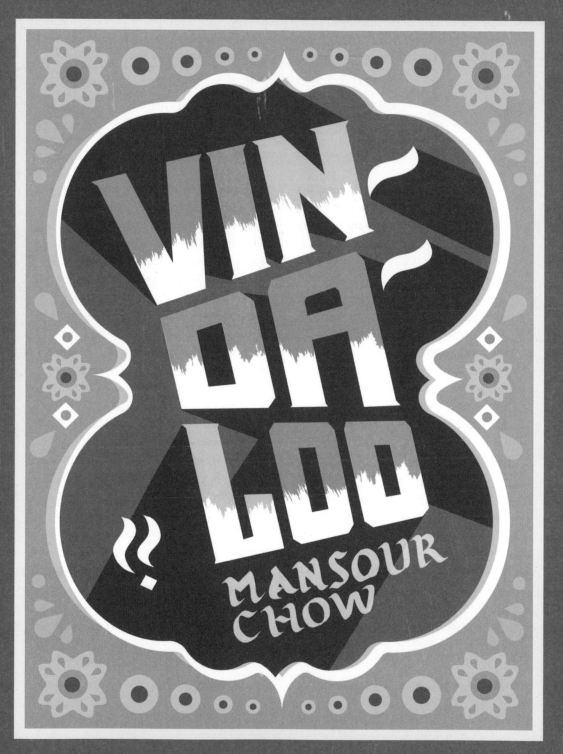

> **When something is so lovely, it can be difficult to accept that it might not be right for us.**

It hurts to accept that we shouldn't have that in our life anymore. It's hard not to crave the immediate pleasure it gives us. But we know, deep down, the pain that follows is too much for us to handle.

The most obvious example of this is addiction to, and craving for, cigarettes. It's a nice buzz, a pick-up, a calming influence. But afterwards, it makes us irritable, it weakens our lungs; and it's cancerous. Thankfully, I've never been partial to cigarettes. I have, however, had a long-standing love affair with vindaloo, ending eventually in a sorrowful divorce.

If it hadn't been for significant improvements in ship design in the 15th century, we would know nothing of either cigarettes or vindaloo. Carracks and caravels were Iberian-built ships better suited for long journeys and difficult waters. They incorporated new wind and sail technologies and, most importantly, the carrack was sufficiently roomy for large scale intercontinental trades.

In the search for spices and with the desire to increase trade between the continents, Christopher Columbus and his crew set sail for India in a carrack, and inadvertently stumbled upon the Americas. They mistakenly thought they had reached their destination, having witnessed the natives using chilli peppers, assuming they were the spices they were after. The journey to the Americas ended up being how most parents feel about an unplanned baby — a fabulous mistake.

Columbus and his men returned to Europe with chilli peppers and tobacco leaves as a parting gift from the natives. In return for their generosity, Columbus and his crew took part in, and encouraged the rest of Europe in, a mass rape of the natives' land. If you were as baleful as I am, you might say cancer from tobacco would be a fitting consequence for those men.

Due to the new faster and larger ships, the world had become smaller, and intercontinental trade increased to the point that the real India was discovered and first introduced to the chilli pepper in the late 15th century. Chilli peppers were cheaper than ordinary peppers, and the Indian climate was well-suited to growing them.

The etymology of vindaloo is often thought, wrongly, to be the simple blend of wine (*vin*) and potatoes (*aloo*). The dish actually started from the Portuguese influx into Goa after their successful invasion in 1510. The name is derived from a common Portuguese dish named *Carnes De Vinha D'Alhos* (or rather unimaginatively in English, 'meat of garlic wine') and the cuisine evolved in its journey through India to become the spicy vindaloo curry we know today. The addition of potatoes most likely came as result of the expense of lamb and to bulk the dish up a bit, but the most important change didn't occur until it had reached Mumbai when Kashmiri chillies were added, giving it the look and the taste we now know.

It's surprising that a key ingredient in one of the most famed Indian dishes is not actually indigenous to the area. Despite the surprise this might cause, it's not so uncommon. Italy is famed for its tomato-based cuisine, but the tomato had never actually grown there until after it was discovered in the Americas in the early 16th century. Most Italians had never even seen a tomato until the mid 1500s, when they were grown for ornamental and aesthetic value. But just as the chilli pepper was perfectly suited to the Indian climate, the Italian climate favoured the tomato and it eventually flourished to become the prerequisite staple in the majority of Italy's famed national dishes. It took a while, mind you. The first record of Italians using tomatoes in their cuisine came over 150 years after it was first brought to their shores.

Vindaloo is a beautiful dish. Simple but elegant, with origins rich and complex. And I love it. It may well be the perfect dish, but I've realised that it's not the perfect dish for me. Each time I have vindaloo, I am filled with joy and delight, only to suffer the next day (sometimes even sooner) from a reaction to the ingredient which helps makes it so lovely. Despite how lovely that vindaloo was at the time, I endure such misery afterwards that I can't help but feel regret. Sometimes, as much as we love something, we have to acknowledge it might be worse for us to have it. Sometimes, for our own sake, we have to walk away. F&K

WHERE KWIK SAVES GO TO DIE - FORAGING FOR FOOD IN BIRKENHEAD

RALPH BULLIVANT

As you drive around Tranmere or the north end of Birkenhead, do not be surprised if you come across an old Kwik Save store still open for business, forgotten to close down, doors standing open on half empty shelves stacked with rusty tins of No Frills Baked Beans selling at 7p a tin, no longer stacking it high but still selling it cheap, red and white labelled plastic bags flapping by the dust covered tills and old cardboard boxes, waiting to take your shopping home. The Kwik Saves have gone, of course, boarded up and closed for business, another decline in a part of the country where blasts of economic cold air follow quickly one after another.

Sitting at a desk five days a week, there is little or no opportunity to shop for good food. So Saturday mornings at home in Birkenhead take on a special importance: the few hours in the week when I have a chance to root through boxes of vegetables and fruit, speak to butchers and fishmongers and ferret through shelves of harissa, chickpeas and rice.

Around Birkenhead the end of terraces still carry the faded lettering of old painted adverts, sometimes half blocked by a new building, Morgan's Spiced Gin, CHEMIST, Fothergill's Haberdashery, in faded white paint on a slate roof, raised tiled lettering in red: BAKERY 1900 on Balls Road next to the brash sign for Strippers: You Name It! We'll Strip It!

I travel a well-worn path along the north side of the Wirral, where Birkenhead sits opposite its bigger and more imposing sister Liverpool, on a regular weekend mission to fill my bags with the ingredients for the soup for Saturday lunch, evening supper and a late lunch on Sunday. The journey starts down Oxton Road, past the motorcycle shop bearing two terracotta panels announcing that this was the site of the BIRKENHEAD BREWERY COMPANY LTD 1896.

Almost directly opposite is K & N Fresh Vegetables & Fruit. Nader and Karem are originally from Iran, but have lived in, Liverpool, for the last 30 years. The 1970s small business unit is stripped back to basics: a red concrete floor, two rows of shelving down each side, two small fridges and a central area filled with boxes of apples, banana, pears. Pick up a basket from the untidy stack in the corner and fill it with dirty beetroot, potatoes and carrots, tomatoes that look like they have seen some sun, £2.99 for a cardboard tray. Four different shapes of aubergine: great black bulbs as thick as a fist, smaller ones as long as a finger, thin purple and white as long as a finger, thin purple and white striped; bags of English apples; proper green spinach grown down the road in Hoylake, done up with string in bunches of hard green metallic flavour.

Behind the counter there is a broken radio tied to the wall. As the bags are packed to the sound of light classics, Nader is careful to put the hard stuff at the bottom so the more delicate tomatoes and soft fruit are not squashed. Next to the till, a petition for the council to plant some trees down Oxton Road. The council have blown hot and cold about it, although more recently someone new has come down to talk to Karem and sounded more positive. As Karem says, it wouldn't take much to plant a few trees and their blossom in spring would help to transform the road. 2000 people signed the petition. If the look of the road could be improved it would attract more people and then maybe more shops would open and the roller shutters could be pushed up. A grocer needs a butcher, fishmonger and baker to be next to it and then people would come rather than relying on Tesco or Sainsbury's.

Karem talks a new Saturday girl through what she has to do. It is all in the look, the piles of fresh veg and fruit on the shelves, nothing brown or mottled, as soon as that happens it needs to be taken off, and as far as possible the shelves should be kept full, no empty spaces. The old stuff is not thrown away, but bagged up and put on the 50p shelf where bargains can be had if you are careful.

Early on a Saturday morning there are loaves of brown bread baked by a German baker in Speke, ducks eggs, sold by the half dozen, fresh asparagus tips, downy figs wrapped in tissue paper, cherries and, in season, honey mangoes from Pakistan, small and yellow, the skin slightly wrinkled, sold wrapped in shredded blue paper in boxes of four, tied with a ribbon. They smell of honey. Later, their orange flesh will be slippery and sweet, perfect after a heavy, spiced meal.

Drop the first bag of shopping in the car in the deserted car park at the back of the casino, one of the few new buildings on Oxton Road where the only colour to be found is in the different shades of grey in the roller shutters and the shop front of Norman E Marriott 'Brushes & mops, buckets & bowls'. Bright green, caged windows hung with the same three hard brushes that have been there for the ten years I have been driving past, a hardware store selling toilet tissue by the roll, and one window looking into tables of dried flowers, old board games amongst the bric-à-brac for sale. Norman Marriott still sits behind his hand-cranked till, occasionally standing to shuffle his stock around before sitting back down and waiting for his next customer.

Carry on down Oxton Road to Charing Cross and the Grange Shopping Centre. Grange Electrical on the right, a blizzard of dated white goods, piles of proper light bulbs in the window. Sadly Siam the small Thai shop has closed. The lady who ran it may never have got over mistaking my 16-year-old daughter for my wife. They always had a fridge cabinet of Thai veg: red shallots, lemongrass, beans three foot long, galangal, pea sized aubergines, packets of strange greens that I would buy without being sure what they were.

Heading for Birkenhead Market, you pass Skeleton Records and the thumps from the dance studio on the first floor above the nail salon and over Charing Cross, where the pubs open at 10am, with windows that open onto to the road so you can lean out with your pint and elbows watching the world whorl by in a blur of Carling and black, a busy McDonald's on the corner and into the murk of the Grange Precinct, an old man in a flowery shirt sitting on a plastic chair, taking tips for plucking along on a tennis racket to a tinny cassette.

Marks & Spencer had one of their first stalls in the original market, opened in 1835. Hard to think now that there was a first stall, but you never know: there may be something going on amid the kiosks selling cheap shoes, foam, pet food, bright clothes for a Saturday night and always the biggest queue at the stall doing school uniforms. The market still has a small corner given over to food, and that is where I am heading.

Beryl's Plaice. Beryl has had 32 years of experience in the fish trade. Fresh Scottish Fish delivered every day. Fish can be skinned and boned to suit any requirements. Suppliers to Nursing Homes and restaurants. Ward's Fish is next, in the middle of a row of four fish stalls. They have been up since early in the morning, at the wholesale fish market on Edge Lane, a great Victorian barn hanging on in the 21st century. The business was started by Simon and Nigel's great-grandmother; it has followed the mothers through the years until its present incarnation. If I am making fish soup it pays to get there early for a bag of bones and a good fish head, hake with its awful leopard teeth or halibut that Victorian giant of the Icelandic

YES, IT WOULD HAVE BEEN EASIER TO HAVE DONE ALL THAT IN THE CONVENIENCE OF ONE SUPERMARKET.

deep. Or red mullet, the most beautiful of fish, so cook it for someone you love. It does not have the slick metallic sheen of mackerel, but there is dirty gold in the pink skin, and part of the trick in cooking it is to preserve some of that skin for its colour on the plate. On the right of the fridge cabinet for the fish there is usually a great silver tray of salt cod. They were making their own years ago but could never quite sell enough to make it worthwhile. Then Peter Kinsella opened Lunya in Liverpool One, cooking up some of the best Catalan food in the country, and he needed good salt cod for his salt cod *buñuelos*, a tapas bar favourite: salt cod, parsley, garlic and mashed potato, deep fried and served with *allioli*.

Once I have a bag of fish from Ward's, I start on the walk back up Oxton Road to the International Store. Here there is flatbread and proper pitta; shelves of my favourite thin green peppers, clean, crisp and hot; and then into the depths of the shop, four or five rows of shelving neatly ordered, glass jars of chickpeas, fat and bulbous Garrdo Garbanzos from Spain, and butter beans, pickled lemons and limes, bags of rice and noodles, dried limes and barberry from Iran, couscous and pistachios, a butcher's at the back,

chickens with the head and feet still on, trays of chillies and ginger, swathes of coriander and parsley, tins of sour cheese from Turkey. Small golden tins of Le Phare du Cap Bon Harissa, de piment rouge fort, sauce piquante de Tunisie, to be smeared on a chicken for roasting the following day and eaten with fried potatoes and tomato sauce. Ghormeh Sabzi, a mixture of dried parsley, chives, fenugreek and coriander leaves used in the making of a rich Iranian beef stew. Strange drinks from Thailand: Ta Ra Basil Seed Drink with Honey, looking like frog spawn in an Orangina bottle, or Jogo de Tamarindo, tamarind juice.

Behind the counter more shelves, strange packets of dye, chipped pestles and mortars, packets of cups and glasses marked in faded brown Arabic. Pea green packets of Psyllium Husk Sat-Isabgol from The Siddhpur Sat-Isabgol Factory on Bindu Sarover Road Our's 65th Year, excessive consumption may produce laxative effects.

Then back to the car for the short drive to New Ferry. Park in the Community Hall car park and walk down to the Old Chester Road past the closed Strut Yr Stuff clothes shop, pawnbrokers with their gold signs and more pubs that open at 10am to a steady trade, computer shops selling second hand black boxes, wires loose. Karaoke with David Stevens as Justin Bieber. One of the pubs is called The John Masefield after the poet laureate who wrote *Sea Fever* – 'I must go down to the sea again'. He spent time in New Ferry before he set off on his travels on the sea. God knows what he would make of it now. The pub sign has given him an unfortunate moustache, so it is nicknamed The Adolf.

And so to Edge & Sons, the butchers. They have been there for six generations and were established in 1844, so John Masefield must have walked under their striped awning on The Old Chester Road as he made his way off to sea. Edge's feels out of place. Customers are still called Sir or Madam; they would be more at home on the high street of an old-fashioned Cheshire village. Any relationship with a good butcher should start with their bacon and sausages. Edge & Sons make their own, home-cured back and middle, sweet-cured streaky, and 13 (the last time I counted) varieties of sausage. They source their meat from three breeds of pig, British Saddleback, Gloucester Old Spot and Middle White, and reassuringly they operate their own abattoir, so if you were to ask they could almost give a name to the animal you are buying your meat from. There is always a good supply of

trotters and the occasional pigs ear, worth, at 50p a time, throwing in to add some heft and depth to a stew; or if I feel like challenging the guests on Sunday, a pigs ear terrine out of the St John's cookbook. Once a year the horseradish plant in the corner of the garden gives up its roots and in the deepening gloom of a late Sunday afternoon we will have roast beef.

Once I am out of Edge's it is a quick rush back to the car and the drive back home listening to something loud and unpleasant on the stereo in the hope there is enough time to make the pot of soup I promised for lunch.

Yes, it would have been easier to have done all that in the convenience of one supermarket. Time would have been saved and perhaps less money spent, although that is a toss up between the more expensive meat and fish versus the cheaper fruit and veg. But there would not have been so much pleasure, there would have been less chat and no opportunity to furtle along a shelf and pick up something unexpected, like the fiery red dragon fruit I am eating now, split in half, scooping out the pale grey flesh speckled with small poppy like seeds, subtly sweet before I go to bed. **F&K**

CRYPTIC CROSSWORD NUMBER 5

by Crucifer

ACROSS

1. Grouse is famously hung here (5)
4. Pure, terminal-free WiFi developed in equipment that first came from China (not Apple or Blackberry) (4,5)
9. Ash Wednesday at last? Girls gad about (9)
10. Accommodation included in reservation (5)
11. Boost given to the bottom feeder (6)
12. '10' was wrongly interpreted as term of endearment (5,3)
14. Recall TLC must be added to creole cooking (9)
16. Girl greedily scoffing sandwiches (5)
17. Rough Latin translation (5)
19. Other turn perversely taken to reach pole position (4,5)
21. American cheese as menu changes on way to queen (8)
22. Northern heavyweight's retro salad, including game (6)
25. Derivative and ultimately pointless dessert (5)
26. Naval engagement in long, tumultuous decline (9)
27. Used to head straight for island formation (6,3)
28. Extreme position of returning executive (one on board) (5)

DOWN

1,5. Suggestion from the 22 and the 15 to 23, perhaps, (according to 3): throw away dustiest monocles when cracked (1,7,4,3,4,4,2)
2. Golfer's G-string discovered outside (5)
3. Reverend in road accident? (7)
4. Rescheduling Ski Sunday is a nice touch (4)
5. See 1dn.
6. Fool combined butter and pate (7)
7. Out to get one kind of musician (9)
8. Harshest wickets prepared for very best (3,4,8)
13. Beckham's position: 'Sinsemilla has it.' (6,4)
15. Go in after fish and chips (9)
18. Land-locked country: another nation in need of a port (7)
20. River rising in northern Arkansas range (7)
23. Spade following diamond is staggering (5)
24. Airline initially banned from production of banana bread (4)

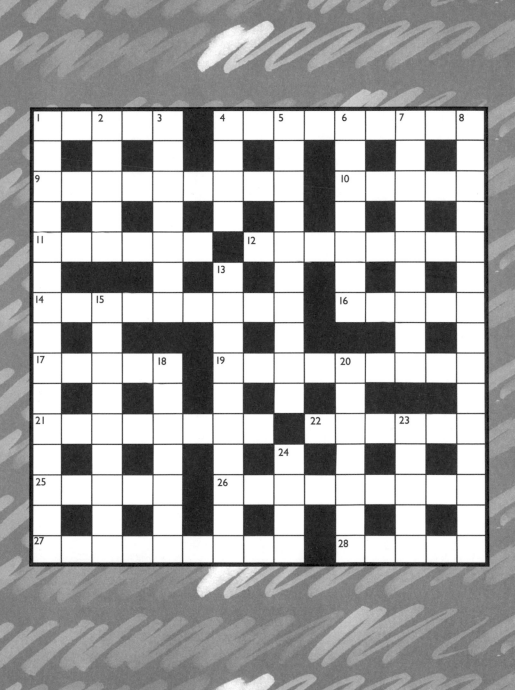

1 B	I	2 G	N	3 I	G	4 H	T		5 W	6 E	A	L	7 T	H	8 H
Y		R		C		I				S			E		E
9 P	L	A	Y	H	O	S	T		10 E	C	L	A	I	R	
A		P		O		W		11 M		A		D			L
12 S	U	P	E	R	S	I	Z	E		13 L	I	M	B	O	
S		A			F		M			O		I		V	
		14 S	15 T	Y	E		16 E	X	P	A	N	S	E		R
17 T		18 T	I				E			E			R		
19 H	A	I	R	P	I	N	20		21 T	O	S	S			
E		F	S		O		H				22 M		23 S		
24 T	A	F	F	Y		25 B	R	E	A	26 K	F	A	S	T	
H		A		C		U		C		R			R		
27 I	O	N	I	A	N		28 C	O	Q	U	E	T	T	E	
E		Y		K				O		P			R		A
29 F	I	S	H	E	S		30 S	K	I	P	J	A	C	K	

The four down entries that were clued without definition were
The Cook, The Thief, His Wife and Her Lover (dir Peter Greenaway, 1989)

Thomas Blythe is a restaurant insider and consultant who writes for *GQ, Port* Magazine and others on a range of topics from eating to the joys of the short back and sides. He also blogs occasionally at ifdogsosmartwhynothedrivecar.wordpress.com

Jonathan Brown is currently working for an advertising agency in Gothenburg where he is enjoying the chance to explore Scandinavian food and culture. He writes the monthly Sandwichist column for the Londonist and blogs about his British and Swedish food experiences at aroundbritainwithapaunch.blogspot.com

Originally from the Wirral peninsula, **Mansour Chow** works and lives in North London. He is co-creator of the dark, silly, twisted, limited edition print literary magazine *The Alarmist*. www.alarmistmagazine.co.uk & Twitter @alarmistmag

Rachael Blyth is an actress, writer and filmmaker from the Shetland Isles. She studied at the University of York and Central Saint Martins before joining London-based theatre company FoolishPeople in 2010. Their first feature film, *Strange Factories*, is currently in post-production. Rachael's writings on culture, film, performance and ritual are regularly published online at foolishpeople.com and elsewhere.

Mark Anstead used to interview celebrities every week for a range of national newspapers. He's recently cut down on that to start Cambridgeshire Wine School because he finds tasting wine, matching with food and writing about it all far more interesting. www.winewithfood.com

Laura Day is a London-based writer who firmly believes that if you can eat it, you should write about it. You can find all of her work relating to food, TV and quite often the two together at thewritingtype.com

Jessica Keath grew up in the wine-growing region of Mclaren Vale and has worked in many areas of the food industry from establishing a restaurant garden at Russell's pizza, to dish-pig at the Star of Greece and front of house at Vue de Monde. Since graduating from acting school in Sydney, she divides her time between freelance writing, acting, teaching 'NIDA Chef' and has recently set the wheels in motion for a wood-fired food truck business.

Judy O'Kane has drawn blood at the chopping board from the kibbutz kitchen to vegetarian classes in India. She recently travelled to New Zealand in pursuit of pinot, qualified from Ballymaloe Cookery School, Cork and worked a harvest in Bordeaux. Judy is a solicitor in Dublin. judyokane@gmail.com

Breil Bistro (@breilbistro) is a food-trend contrarian who is in perpetual search for the holy triptych of good food, cooked well at reasonable prices. He is also hiding behind anonymity to keep his employers happy while he figures out if he's got what it takes to run his own restaurant or bistro or café or food empire.

Stuart Ritson: Barista in practice, Sinologist at heart. Adds Sichuan pepper to everything. Coffee is à la mode but tea is on the horizon.

Mike Sim is a Scottish comedian, writer and front of house dogsbody living and working in Cambridge. When he's not uncorking wine and steaming milk he can be found deconstructing the mundane to crowds often surpassing single figures.

Tom Leahy was born and raised in rural North Yorkshire, but has lived in London for the last six years. His day job involves spreadsheets; however, Tom's real passions are food and drink, skiing and cricket. His writing has been described as 'very enjoyable' on at least three separate occasions. gastrolad.blogspot.com

Ralph Bullivant is a lawyer from Liverpool. He spends time each summer in Ahakista, south-west Cork, where he catches and kills mackerel, buys lobster and crab from Tommy the fisherman and cooks it all for friends and family, washed down with Murphy's from Arundel's Pub. He is writing a book about all this called *How to Kill a Mackerel*.

Brie O'Keefe is an international charity worker by day and food fanatic and blogger by night whose career has taken her to over 35 countries including Liberia and East Timor. *Seal Blood Soup* is her first published short story and is set in Nunavut, a fly-in community of 400 on an island in the middle of the Arctic Ocean.

Josh Sutton cooked his first camping meal at the age of nine, it all went horribly wrong and he burst into tears. Things have improved since then, though the tears do still flow on the odd occasion. He's been writing about cooking & camping for the past three years and has written for *Go Camping Magazine*, *Lakeland Walker* magazine and the Foodie Bugle among others. He is the author of the increasingly popular website www.guyropegourmet.com

Stefan Chomka is an award-wining food journalist (under tens 20-metre backstroke) who is deputy editor of *Restaurant* magazine and who writes for a number of other national food titles. He splits his time equally between eating, drinking and recovering, with the odd bit of writing thrown in for good measure. He has no waist size.

Eleanore Johnson is a South African who has recently completed her Masters in English Literature. Her academic field is ecocriticism, the study of the relationship between literature and nature. *Snoek Bisque* is part of the adaptation of her grandmother's recipe book into a publishable family cookbook, hopefully with its zest and character intact.

Zoh is a Kiwi living happily in Melbourne. In her spare time, she loves discovering and trying out the new food places springing up like mushrooms in Melbourne. The story of Sue and Ren is her first ever short story. She hopes to meet them in real life some day.

THE GAST R ICIAN

Many obituaries have been written for the gentleman's club, and none is right. There may be death seeping through the reading rooms of St James and Pall Mall, where the Chesterfields carry a dust of their members' calcified bone. The In & Out, The Colonial, Tramples, Pontins, The Axminster: all have passed into the portfolio of some odious property speculator with razor burn on his neck. But their passing should not suggest the death of the club. Nothing could be further from the truth.

Macguffins, today's restaurant, is as much a club as any of those historic names. The only difference is that membership is tacit. Though the door appears open to all, hospitality will be extended by invite only. And, if you asked to come in, you were not invited.

London once had two of these places: The Ivy poached eggs for national treasures while Le Caprice fed those living on the backwash of the Civil List. Now there are dozens, all over town, each rationing their tables by an invisible social order. These are the evolution of clubbery, putting the lightest of equitable patinas on their exclusivity. Everyone is welcome, but some are more welcome than others.

So to Macguffins. The restaurant is sited below Bolingbroke Hotel, in a theatre commissioned by Viscount Lepic to stage game fights. The room retains many of the original features from when the venue fell into disuse in 1987. Claw-scratched oak jowls the floorspace, which has been terraced into concentric circles down the theatre's sharp slope. The cloakroom door retains its original brass plate for corgi kennels, and a fresco commemorating the venue's most notable bouts circumcises the lap of The Gods. I am seated next to a mural of the famous contest in 1967 when the Lady Stanhope dispatched an irate peacock with her husband's Beretta.

All that dark wood, tile, burlap and sawdust makes for a room some will consider brutish rather than handsome. But, of course, you are not there for the décor.

First glance at the menu reveals the influence of Europe's grand cafés, where potential for mishap is neutered by favouring construction over cooking. There are salads and carpaccios, an oyster bar, an omelette station, a soup sluice, a doner totem and a crudité sideboard. Pastas also feature, in classic forms such as spaghetti cantori and cloaca stuffed with lovage. The simplicity at work here speaks of a confidence that no-one needs to be impressed.

I ordered a Hot Port Negus and sat back to consider the circumstance. My table in The Gods afforded a privacy that did not extend to those in the circles, where the theatre's incline facilitates the low sport of rubbernecking. Each tightening loop of tables is set a few feet below the last, inviting diners to look up to those above and down on those below. At the centre of the room, in what was once the fighting pit, has been placed a single two-top that on my visit was occupied by the journalist Toby Young.

It is a scene reminiscent of a play without actors. People are buying tickets just to look at the people who buy tickets. Thankfully, the loftiest level allows one to opt out of this spectacle. My own seat near the cornice, behind a pillar and under an air conditioning unit, required neither to see nor be seen. An insecure person would no doubt find more comfort among the murmuration of the lower levels. But, of course, you are not there for the atmosphere.

Dinner proceeded without undue haste.

A quad-baked soufflé had benefited from a lengthy resting between the third and fourth bakings, which had vulcanised its skin to a pleasing ductility. Jugged hamstring (the superior of the *prêt-à-boucher* cuts) was plated rare then brought up to medium by a generous pause under a pass heatlamp. A tarte Tatin to finish had been idling in cold storage for sufficiently long that it had become impossible to tell where tarte stopped and Tatin began.

It is a menu that will not please everyone. Those dazzled by the try-hard pseudoscience of nameplate chefs will find little here to wow. Macguffins instead luxuriates in the comfort of the achievable. Its cuisine is a celebration of the commonplace, like a Barbour jacket or a Tupperware box for your cornflakes. It is,

truth be told, perfectly possible to eat through the menu rather badly. But, of course, you are not there for the food.

And it barely needs noting that demand for Macguffins exceeds supply. This is also true of everywhere you would wish to be.

To the common man, London has become a city where the restaurants that take bookings cannot be booked. The effect is the same. The common man must wait his turn. He can wait three hours in the queue outside a burger bar for a space on the shared bench, or he can wait three months to sit at an unpopular time in the overlooked corner of a room where he doesn't belong.

Such apartheid is unpleasant. It was an unpleasant task for the gentlemen's clubs of Pall Mall and it is just as unpleasant for their successors, who fell upon inconvenience as the most acceptable proxy for a blackball vote. What makes it necessary is that London has too much money, and most of it has gone to the wrong sort of people. We cannot rely on price alone to discriminate, as America does. Instead, we must fall back on the national code of status and standing, class and connection. People need to be kept to their place. And, if the reservations girl puts you on hold, there could be no clearer message that this is not your place.

Critics of Macguffins have failed to understand that the only measure of a castle is the width of its moat. Talk of 'mediocre' food and 'inept' service misses the point, as, once in the right table at the right time, it is still one the most agreeable ways you could spend your evening. But, of course, you are not there. **F&K**

Macguffins
1a Dalrymple Place, W1 1AA
Tel: no.

PIE   LATTICE   TART